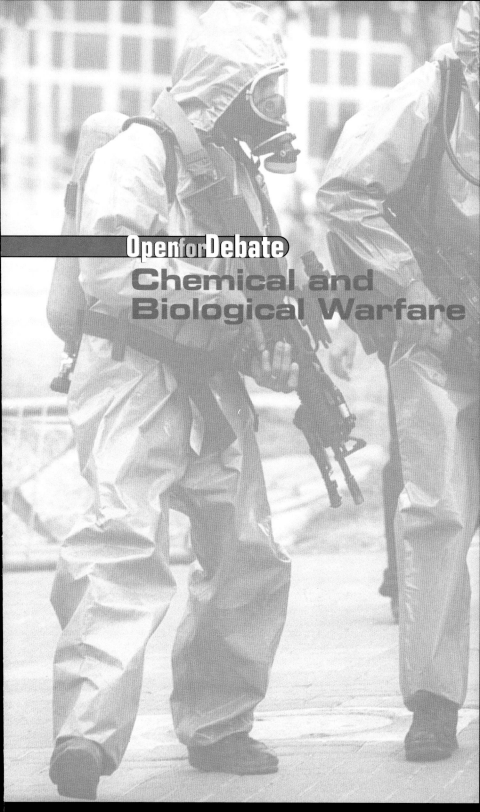

Open for Debate
Chemical and
Biological Warfare

Open for Debate

Chemical and Biological Warfare

Karen Judson

BENCHMARK BOOKS

MARSHALL CAVENDISH
NEW YORK

With thanks to Gigi Kwik, Ph.D., Fellow at the Center for
Civilian Biodefense Strategies, Johns Hopkins University,
for her expert review of this manuscript.

Benchmark Books
Marshall Cavendish
99 White Plains Road
Tarrytown, NY 10591-9001
www.marshallcavendish.com

All Internet sites were available and accurate when sent to press.

Library of Congress Cataloging-in-Publication Data
Judson, Karen, 1941-
Biological and chemical warfare / by Karen Judson.
p. cm. -- (Open for debate)
Includes bibliographical references and index.
Contents: The poor man's atom bomb--The bioterror attacks of 2001--
The major biological weapons and their effects--The major chemical weapons and their
effects--History and uses of chemical and biological weapons--Tests and accidents --
Developing protection for soldiers--Control and disarmament--Cheaters and remedies --
Protecting ourselves and ridding the world of chemical and biological weapons.
ISBN 0-7614-1585-8
1. Biological warfare--Juvenile literature. 2. Chemical warfare--Juvenile literature.
[1. Biological warfare.
2. Chemical warfare.] I. Title. II. Series.
UG447.8.J83 2004
358'.38--dc21

2003007768
Photo Research by Linda Sykes Picture Research, Inc., Hilton Head, SC

AFP/Corbis: Cover, 2, 3–4, 6; AP/WideWorld Photos: 11; Steve Mitchell/AP/WideWorld
Photos: 25; Sipa Press: 31(left), 31(right), 40, 51, 66; Asahi Shimbun/Sipa Press: 56;
Ozturk/Sipa Press: 61; Imperial War Museum/The Art Archive: 67; Lennox
McLendon/AP/WideWorld Photos: 86; Corbis: 91; IAEA/Sipa Press: 108; Stephen
Chernin/AP/Wide World Photos: 117.

Printed in China

1 3 5 6 4 2

**COVER: DURING A TRAINING MISSION ON NOVEMBER 14, 2001, ISRAELI
POLICEMEN WEARING CHEMICAL AND BIOLOGICAL WARFARE PROTECTIVE SUITS
EVACUATED A SIMULATED INJURED PERSON IN THE ISRAELI TOWN OF REUT,
EAST OF TEL AVIV.**

Contents

"Man's inhumanity to man
"Makes countless thousands mourn!"
Robert Burns (1759–1796)

1

The Poor Man's Atomic Bomb

It was a warm, sunny Saturday in mid-February, and many of the men, women, and children of Kansas City, Missouri, were outside enjoying the unexpected mid-winter thaw. Because of the unseasonably warm weather, malls were packed with shoppers. Some of the shoppers had driven in from nearby towns, more to enjoy the break in the weather than to fill their shopping bags. At the giant Metro Mall, not one of the thousands of shoppers or shop clerks noticed what appeared to be a video-cassette-sized canister taped to a wall near the food court, nor should they have been expected to notice such an ordinary object.

Within a few days after the February thaw, many people called in sick to work or school, suffering from backaches, stomachaches, and fever. A flu epidemic had begun two weeks before, so most patients who saw their doctors or reported to hospital emergency rooms were sent home with a diagnosis of flu and told to rest, drink plenty of fluids, and take over-the-counter pain medications.

Crystal Green, a local high school English teacher, was one of those patients. She followed her doctor's advice, but her condition grew worse. Soon after she saw her doctor, Green's fever had risen, she was nauseous, and her face had broken out in a red rash. Although Green felt sicker than she had ever felt with the flu, she stayed in bed and hoped the symptoms would soon pass. When the rash on her face changed to pus-filled blisters that hardened and burned, and the pain in her abdomen was no longer bearable, Green asked her husband to take her to a nearby hospital emergency room. The emergency room, like ERs throughout the city, was flooded with patients who suffered from high fevers, painful skin blisters, and severe abdominal pain.

Because the last case of smallpox in the United States had occurred in 1949, and the last outbreak of the disease occurred in Somalia in 1977, most of the doctors treating patients in Kansas City's hospital emergency rooms, clinics, and doctors' offices had no idea what to call the disease they were seeing. One physician in Green's hospital emergency room, however, had just returned from a government-sponsored seminar on chemical and biological weapons, so she knew smallpox when she saw it. By the time the cases were diagnosed, though, the highly contagious disease had spread rapidly and almost 15 percent of the city's 1,663,000 residents were ill.

Soon after the epidemic began in Kansas City, public health authorities there called for a massive smallpox vaccination program for all medical workers, those showing early symptoms of the disease and their contacts, and finally for everyone else. But routine smallpox vaccinations for American children and adults had ended in 1972 when the disease was thought to have been wiped out worldwide, so very little smallpox vaccine had been produced since. Despite the fact that Kansas City residents were told they must wait for smallpox vaccine to be flown in, most *remained calm and monitored news sources for information about vaccine availability. Residents were asked to stay in their homes and not to leave for any reason in order to avoid passing the disease to others.*

Schools and businesses closed when students, teachers, and workers became too ill to leave their homes. City services, such as garbage pick-up, newspaper delivery, meter reading, meals-on-wheels for seniors, buses and taxis, came to a standstill. Movie theaters were closed, school athletic events were cancelled, and all professional sports, drama, and musical events were postponed. As an increasing number of people died from the disease, even burying the dead became a problem because those who normally performed these duties were either at home, sick with smallpox, or afraid to leave home for fear of catching the disease.

Each smallpox patient infected at least ten others, and when the scourge had run its course 30 percent of the city's population was dead. Millions of smallpox cases were also reported in twenty-five other states, and in Canada, Mexico, and Europe, as well. At least a third of those patients would die. Those who survived would be scarred for life. Crystal Green survived the disease, but it would be several weeks before she felt strong enough to return to work.

As the epidemic raged through Kansas City and moved outward, no one noticed a man in the Metro Mall dressed in janitor's coveralls who removed what appeared to be a thermostat from a wall near the food court. He pocketed the device and then he casually walked out of the mall. He smiled as he drove from the parking lot, exited to the interstate highway, and headed out of state.

The above scenario is fiction. It is similar, however, to an exercise sponsored by the Johns Hopkins Center for Civilian Biodefense Strategies on June 22 and 23, 2001, in collaboration with the Center for Strategic and International

Studies, the Anser Services Institute for Homeland Security, and the Oklahoma City National Memorial Institute for the Prevention of Terrorism. The exercise, called "Dark Winter," simulated a smallpox attack on the United States that originated in Oklahoma City, Oklahoma, instead of in Kansas City as fictionalized here. Dark Winter assumed the United States had not prepared to protect against a biological attack and was taken completely by surprise.

For the following reasons, participants in the Dark Winter exercise determined that the fictional, unexpected eruption of smallpox in Oklahoma City was the result of a terrorist attack:

- **there were too many cases showing up at once;**
- **at first, the outbreak was localized;**
- **the disease had been absent in populations for too long a time for this to be a chance infection.**

According to the script for the scenario, the virus was probably released as an aerosol spray in several shopping malls.

The Dark Winter exercise revealed that such an act of terrorism against an unprepared population would not only kill a large percentage of that population, it would also leave the United States without sufficient supplies of vaccine and antibiotics to help those who were exposed to a disease organism or who became ill. Even a 10 percent increase in the number of hospital patients would strain most hospitals beyond their capacities. Health care workers could be in short supply as workers elected to stay home rather than expose friends and family to the highly contagious disease. Many businesses would be forced to close until the epidemic passed. The work interruption would cause nationwide shortages. The shortages and closures would affect business profits and the stock market, and disrupt the nation's economy for many months.

Participants in the exercise also theorized that the epidemic could cause people to panic. This would threaten civil liberties and put undo strain on law enforcement agencies. Studies have shown, however, that in emergencies people do not always panic and thus hinder the efforts of others to help them. In fact, according to "Bioterrorism and the People: How to Vaccinate a City Against Panic," an article by Thomas A. Glass and Monica Schoch-Spana that appeared in the January 15, 2002, issue of *Clinical Infectious Diseases*, in the past the public has responded effectively

A Thai soldier wearing a gas mask signals other participants during a chemical warfare training exercise conducted jointly with the United States military in Sattahip, Thailand, on May 16, 2002. The purpose of the exercise was to practice anti-terrorism measures and the evacuation of military personnel and civilians during emergencies.

to disasters, including the 1918 Spanish flu epidemic, the 1947 smallpox outbreaks in New York City, and the September 11, 2001, terrorist attacks on the World Trade Center and the Pentagon. "Standards of civil behavior prevail even in the most challenging circumstances," the authors state. "Resourceful, adaptive behavior is the rule rather than the exception in communities beset by technological and natural disasters as well as epidemics," they conclude.

Lessons learned during and after the Dark Winter exercise allowed government agencies and public health authorities to begin detailed planning for dealing with such a crisis in the United States. Similar terrorist-response training exercises conducted in Seattle, Chicago, and Washington, D.C., in May 2003 also provided valuable information to U.S. government agencies that would be the first to respond to terrorist attacks.

Federal and state public health departments play a large part in maintaining readiness for biological attacks. Normally, public health departments work to control disease by:

1. Protecting the public against unsanitary conditions in public places;

2. Inspecting businesses where food and drink are processed and sold;

3. Getting rid of pests and vermin, such as flies and rats, that can spread disease;

4. Checking water quality;

5. Requiring health practitioners, teachers, and others to report certain diseases;

6. Setting up measures, such as immunization clinics, to control certain diseases.

In emergency situations, such as attacks with biological weapons, public health departments would be valuable sources of information and assistance. Therefore, after the Dark Winter exercise, state and federal governments worked to improve disease-response measures:

- **The federal government ordered more smallpox and anthrax vaccine from drug companies. The government also began stockpiling certain drugs for the treatment of disease;**

- **Cities were asked to establish disaster plans for chemical and biological warfare emergencies that would include improving communication and surveillance systems;**

- **Health care workers were better trained to recognize smallpox, anthrax, and other diseases not commonly seen in the United States;**

- **Medical practitioners learned how to treat diseases most likely to be caused by biological warfare and illnesses as well as injuries caused by toxic chemicals;**

- **Plans would be made for setting up medical aid stations and other emergency centers in heavily populated areas;**

- **Public health departments nationwide would receive more funds for personnel, supplies, and computerized tracking and warning systems;**

- **The federal government asked public health departments in each state to prepare detailed plans for reaching the ill or injured and their contacts, in case** of a communicable disease epidemic. Public health officials also needed to work out plans with hospitals for handling more patients in need of isolation, and for distributing drugs provided by the federal government;

• The federal government also asked that the nationwide public health reporting system be improved. For example, when an unusually large amount of a certain drug is sold by a pharmaceutical facility, public health departments will be notified. Unusual events that were not reported before, such as authorities finding more dead animals on the streets, or more students absent from school, will be reported to public health authorities.

In December 2002, President George W. Bush announced a nationwide smallpox vaccination program for protecting all Americans. Under the plan, the Department of Health and Human Services (HHS) would work with state and local governments to form volunteer Smallpox Response Teams. These teams would be made up of police and fire personnel, emergency and health care workers and any others who would most likely be first to come into contact with people exposed to smallpox. Smallpox Response Teams would be vaccinated against smallpox first. As of May 2003, Smallpox Response Team personnel had been offered the vaccine.

The federal smallpox vaccination program is a pre-event program, meaning that vaccinations are to be given before any smallpox cases appear. Initially the government hoped to vaccinate approximately 500,000 health care workers in the first phase of the program, followed by a second phase of vaccination of an additional 10 million health care and other emergency personnel.

The federal government did not recommend vaccination for the general public yet, since there was no reason to believe that smallpox presented an immediate threat. If any member of the general public insisted, however, he or she would be vaccinated.

The president also announced that the Department of Defense would vaccinate certain military and civilian personnel who were serving in high threat areas, or might be sent to such areas. As commander in chief of the U.S. Armed Forces, President George W. Bush was one of the first to be vaccinated against smallpox.

By December 2002, the government had acquired enough smallpox vaccine to vaccinate every single American in case of an emergency. The voluntary vaccination of Smallpox Response Teams personnel was begun nationwide in February 2003, but by the end of that month few people had volunteered, perhaps due to fears of medical complications from the vaccine.

Along with nuclear weapons, chemical and biological weapons have been classified as weapons of mass destruction (WMD). These weapons are also known by the easy-to-remember acronym NBC (Nuclear, Biological and Chemical weapons). Because chemical and biological weapons are generally less expensive to acquire than nuclear weapons, they have been called the "poor man's atomic bomb." (Some sources say the phrase "poor man's atomic bomb" originated with Iranian President Ali Akbar Hashemi Rafsanjani in 1988, when Iran was at war with Iraq. It is unclear whether Rafsanjani meant chemical weapons, biological weapons, or both, but the phrase has been used to refer to either or both types of weapons.) An atomic bomb is, of course, a nuclear bomb.

Some experts say that chemical and biological weapons are more accurately categorized as weapons of mass casualties

(WMC), because they are in many ways unlike nuclear weapons. Chemical and biological weapons (CBWs):

• **are not high-tech devices (although their delivery systems may be);**

• **usually do not kill millions swiftly, with one attack, while a nuclear bomb could kill 1 million people outright and many more millions by radiation poisoning over days, weeks, months, and even years after radiation exposure;**

• **do not destroy buildings and infrastructure, although they may make them too dangerous to use for a while, until they are decontaminated (and decontamination can cost billions);**

• **fade away quickly, unlike radiation, which lingers for generations. (Biological organisms that form spores can live for long periods of time and chemicals that stick to foliage and other objects are difficult to clear from an area, but radiation lasts far longer.)**

Chemical and biological agents are attractive weapons to terrorists and even the military troops of various nations for several reasons:

1. The organisms or chemical ingredients are widely available—more so than the elements needed to produce nuclear weapons. Organisms can be bought or stolen, or cultured after a natural disease outbreak. Ordinary house and garden chemicals can be turned into lethal weapons if the "recipe" is known.

2. They are cheap to produce, compared to conventional weapons or nuclear devices.

3. They are easy to conceal because they are spread within a population.

The objectives in using chemical and biological weapons certainly include killing people, but another primary objective is to generate panic and chaos leading to overstressed public health and security systems and to economic instability. Chemical and biological weapons are ideal for accomplishing these objectives. (Nuclear weapons would kill many more people, but to date they are more difficult to acquire and produce.)

Biological weapons are used to deliberately spread disease among humans, animals, and plants. Bioweapons of choice include several disease-causing strains of bacteria, viruses, and fungi. Toxins produced by some organisms, such as botulinum, may also be used, instead of the organism itself.

Chemical weapons are defined as "chemical substances, whether gaseous, liquid or solid, which might be employed because of their direct toxic effects on man, animals and plants." Chemical weapons include several groups of toxic chemicals, classified according to their effects on the human body or on animals and plants. Examples include mustard gas, Agent Orange, and nerve agents such as tabun, sarin, or VX, as discussed in Chapter 4. (The acronym "VX" supposedly stands for "extremely virulent.")

Chemical and biological weapons have been used by nations fighting wars and by groups who are not fighting as military in a declared war, but nevertheless consider themselves soldiers in a cause. These persons are generally called terrorists.

Before they decide to use chemical or biological

weapons, terrorist groups or individuals must have reasons, however misguided or mistaken those reasons may seem to others. Generally, motivation derives from these categories:

- **State-sponsored terrorism. State-sponsored terrorists are funded, trained, and controlled by national governments, and are sent to attack enemies of the state. For example, Iraq allegedly tried to send terrorists to act against the United States during the 1991 Gulf War, but was unsuccessful. And North Korea has been accused of using terrorist groups against South Korea.**

- **Nationalistic or ethnic terrorism. Nationalistic terrorism occurs when groups within a country want to establish a new government, but do not have the troops or resources to wage a full-scale war against the government in power. Examples include the Irish Republican Army (IRA) in Northern Ireland, Palestinian terrorism in the Middle East, and Basque terrorism in Spain.**

- **Ideological terrorism. These terrorist groups or individuals commit acts of terrorism in the name of religious or political agendas. Some groups that fit this category are fanatically extreme animal-rights or anti-abortion groups and religious cults.**

- **Anti-government terrorism. Anti-government terrorists simply wish to attack the government in power, causing damage without setting up their own government to replace it. Timothy McVeigh, who bombed the Alfred P. Murrah Federal building in Oklahoma City on April 19, 2001, killing 168 men, women, and children,** would fit this description. (McVeigh was executed for his crimes by lethal injection at the federal prison in Terre Haute, Indiana, on June 11, 2001.)

• **Psychosis-induced terrorism.** Sometimes an individual is simply mentally unbalanced and follows an agenda of terror known only to himself or herself. If such an individual also has access, or can gain access, to chemical or biological weapons, that person could decide to use them.

Although chemical and biological weapons are attractive to those terrorist groups that do not have the necessary resources to purchase conventional or nuclear weapons, or who simply want to cause death and fear outside of a declared war, there are certain hazards and disadvantages to the use of these weapons:

• an inexperienced person might successfully grow a biological organism, but some knowledge of microbiology is generally required to safely handle and disperse dangerous organisms. Chemical weapons may be somewhat easier to put together, but the chemicals are so toxic that some degree of expertise and care is required to handle and store them;

• accidents that occur when handling the organisms or chemicals could kill or injure the handlers. In fact, even scientists trained in microbiology have been accidentally infected when working with biological agents, and chemists have fallen prey to their own mixtures;

• special precautions must be taken to transport and store the biological and chemical agents, so that leakage

"Biological Terrorist or Harmless Eccentric?"

In 1995, Larry Wayne Harris, an army veteran, member of Aryan Nations, and registered microbiologist from Ohio, bought three vials of plague bacteria by mail for about $300 from a biological supply company based in Maryland called American Type Culture Collection (ATCC). There was no law at that time that prevented Harris from obtaining the culture, but he needed a state laboratory license number to get the plague culture, and he misrepresented himself by using the license number of the scientific company where he worked. He falsely claimed he owned his own laboratory and needed the culture to develop an over-the-counter plague antidote.

The culture was shipped, but the ATCC was suspicious of Harris and notified the Centers for Disease Control and Prevention (CDC), a federal agency that regulates possession of disease organisms and many aspects of American health care. Federal and local law enforcement officers confiscated the plague organism from Harris's home and arrested him. After his arrest, Harris told the news media that he and his fellow Aryan Nations members were prepared to use biological weapons against the government and cities if provoked. "If they arrest a bunch of our guys, they get a test tube in the mail," he said. Harris pleaded guilty to mail fraud—the most serious plea possible under existing law. He was sentenced to eighteen months' probation and 200 hours of community service.

Harris was arrested again in February 1998 in Las Vegas, Nevada, on suspicion of possessing anthrax. When he bragged to an informant that he carried enough anthrax to "wipe out the city," the Federal Bureau of Investigation (FBI) took him into custody. Investigators discovered the anthrax he carried in the glove compartment of his car was a harmless veterinary vaccine strain. He was again given probation and sentenced to community service.

Harris maintained after each arrest that he needed the organisms to develop vaccines, in order to protect the American public from biological weapons attacks. He also said that he had worked for the Central Intelligence Agency (CIA) and the FBI, but neither agency had any record of Harris's alleged employment. He was forbidden by the terms of his probation to make such false claims again.

Larry Harris had not killed anyone, but the government considered him dangerous because he had threatened biological attacks, and he knew enough about microbiology to assist some of the radical groups in the United States and elsewhere that might want to mount a biological attack.

does not occur or unfavorable storage conditions exist that will release the agents prematurely or render the agents less toxic or harmless;

• when biological or chemical agents are released into the air, environmental conditions, such as wind, temperature, and exposure to sunlight cannot be controlled, and may affect survival of the organisms and delivery of the organisms or chemicals;

• there are difficulties involved in controlling the agent and protecting one's own troops. For example, sudden high winds could blow anthrax powder, smallpox virus, or nerve gas released in the air and intended for the enemy back on the attackers. Therefore, it is wise for individuals to be vaccinated, if possible, against the organisms they plan to use as weapons and to have antidotes ready for gases used.

Despite international agreements intended to prevent or halt the development of chemical and biological weapons, in 2002, about nine countries had them or were actively seeking them, including Egypt, Iraq, Iran, Libya, Syria, Israel, North Korea, China and Russia. Twelve more were suspected of having them. One hundred countries were said to have the expertise, equipment, and facilities necessary to create their own.

The possibility of facing biological or chemical attacks by terrorists or hostile military forces is scary. But staying calm and becoming armed with knowledge about biological and chemical weapons is a good defense. The following chapters discuss the effects of chemical and biological weapons, their history and present status, ways to protect against such attacks, and options available to nations that want to rid the world of such weapons.

2

The Bioterror
Attacks of 2001

Americans were reeling after September 11, 2001, when
Islamic fundamentalist terrorists hijacked four commercial
airplanes and crashed two of them into both towers of the
World Trade Center in New York City, one into the Pentagon in Washington, D.C., and the last into a field in Pennsylvania. (The plane that crashed in Pennsylvania was
reportedly headed for the White House, but the hijackers
seem to have been foiled by the passengers, so the plane
crashed instead of hitting its alleged target.) About 3,000
people were killed on that fateful day, and millions in the
United States and elsewhere in the world grieved for the
victims and feared that the terrorists would strike again.

Shortly after the September terrorist attacks, Robert
Stevens, a photo editor at American Media Incorporated
(AMI) in Boca Raton, Florida, took time off from work
for a few days. On September 27, 2001, he left for North

Carolina. His trip had barely begun when, on September 30, Stevens felt so ill that he canceled the remainder of it and returned to his home in Lantana, Florida. Stevens was suffering from a 102-degree fever, vomiting, and confusion when he checked himself into the JFK Medical Center in Atlantis, Florida, at 2:30 A.M. on October 2. Over the next few days his condition deteriorated rapidly, and his body's circulatory and respiratory systems began to shut down. Despite being placed on a respirator and treated with intravenous penicillin, Stevens died on October 5. After his death, the doctors who had treated Stevens diagnosed his illness as an inhaled form of a disease called anthrax. His death was unusual. In fact, he was the first person to die from anthrax in the United States since 1976. Most of the doctors practicing medicine in the United States in 2001 had never seen a case of inhalation anthrax.

Anthrax is a disease caused by a rod-shaped bacterium, *bacillus anthracis.* The name comes from "anthrakis," the Greek word for coal, because when the disease infects a person's skin it can cause black lesions to form. Anthrax bacteria need a warm, moist environment with plenty of food in order to multiply, but the bacteria can lie dormant in soil for decades in the form of spores. Spores are bits of the bacteria's deoxyribonucleic acid (DNA) covered with a tough protein coat. This tough outer coat allows the organism to survive for long periods of time when conditions for it to feed and multiply are absent. When growth conditions are present, as in a human body, the spores are reconverted to rods and the living bacteria begin to reproduce.

Anthrax is found naturally in soil. It usually infects hoofed animals, but seldom people. When humans are infected, they have different immune responses; therefore, people who inhale anthrax spores are affected in different ways. For example, some humans could become ill and even die after inhaling ten spores, while others could inhale

IN OCTOBER 2001, AT AMERICAN MEDIA INCORPORATED (AMI) IN BOCA RATON, FLORIDA, FBI AGENTS AND BOCA RATON FIRE AND RESCUE PERSONNEL INVESTIGATE ANTHRAX CONTAMINATION WITHIN THE AMI BUILDING AFTER THE DEATH OF AMI EMPLOYEE ROBERT STEVENS. STEVENS DIED OF INHALATION ANTHRAX HE WAS EXPOSED TO AT WORK.

10,000 spores before becoming ill. Anthrax spores are microscopic, so they can easily enter the alveoli (small air sacs) inside the lungs.

Anthrax is not contagious—that is, an individual cannot catch the disease from a person who has the disease or has been exposed to it. In cases where people have become infected naturally, they have usually eaten contaminated meat or worked with animals in some way, such as in a veterinary office, raised cattle, sheep, or goats, or they have processed hides, or handled raw meat.

There are three types of anthrax, determined by the means of infection:

1. Cutaneous. Infection occurs through a cut or other open area in the skin that may not be visible to the naked eye.

2. Gastrointestinal. Infection occurs through the ingestion of infected meat.

3. Inhalation or pulmonary. Infection occurs through inhalation of spores.

Once a person has come in contact with anthrax spores, it takes from six to forty-five days to develop the disease. (This is called the incubation period.) All three versions of anthrax cause a high fever. In cutaneous anthrax a red skin rash develops that may eventually turn into black lesions. Gastrointestinal anthrax causes flulike symptoms and, in advanced cases, severe diarrhea and bloody stools and vomitus (material ejected from the stomach during vomiting). All forms of anthrax can be fatal if left untreated, but the inhaled form of the disease usually kills more quickly because the respiratory system is affected, and toxins produced by the multiplying bacteria cause the body's systems to shut down. If caught early, all forms of the disease can be treated with antibiotics. Antibiotics that are usually effective against anthrax include penicillin, Doxycycline and Ciprofloxacin (Cipro).

There is a vaccine for anthrax, but for full protection it must be given before symptoms of the disease appear.

Vaccinating people who have been exposed to anthrax, but have not yet developed symptoms, does not shorten the course of the disease. It does, however, help ensure that late-germinating spores in an exposed person will face a fortified immune system response. In normal times, the military, research scientists, and people who work with animals in occupations where they could come in contact with anthrax are vaccinated, but not the general public.

Shortly before Robert Stevens' hospitalization at JFK Medical Center in October 2001, another employee at AMI fell ill. Ernesto Blanco, seventy-three, worked in the mailroom. He was hospitalized October 1 with what appeared to be pneumonia, but turned out to be inhalation anthrax. While Blanco was hospitalized, his boss at AMI called Blanco's doctor, Carlos Omenaca, at Cedars Medical Center in Miami, to tell him that Stevens had been diagnosed with inhalation anthrax. After this telephone call, Omenaca researched anthrax for six hours. He started Blanco on Cipro and removed bloody fluid from his lungs. The antibiotic killed the bacteria, but the toxins produced by the bacteria continued to cause problems in Blanco's body. At one point Blanco was near death, but his condition finally improved. Omenaca performed tests to prove anthrax had been the cause of Blanco's illness. For example, a nasal swab showed the presence of anthrax spores in Blanco's nose. After twenty-three days of hospitalization, including time spent in intensive care, Blanco was discharged from the hospital on October 23, 2001.

Five other AMI employees—out of hundreds of those employed—contracted the cutaneous form of anthrax. They took Cipro and recovered.

Because finding several cases of anthrax in the same

building is extremely rare, investigators from Florida's state health department and the Centers for Disease Control and Prevention (CDC), based in Atlanta, Georgia, tried to determine the source of the infections. At first they thought Stevens might have come into contact with anthrax spores from the soil during his vacation. This theory was soon discarded because of the time it takes for the disease to develop after one is exposed to the spores. Investigators began to concentrate on the AMI building after Blanco became ill. They found spores on the computer keyboard Robert Stevens used at work and set out to find their source.

Employees who worked near Robert Stevens recalled an unusual letter from an anonymous reader, professing undying love for film star Jennifer Lopez. Since AMI publishes *The National Enquirer, Sun, Star, Globe, Examiner,* and *The Weekly World News* supermarket tabloids, employees had become accustomed to receiving strange letters from readers of the publications. This time, however, they remembered that the letter about Jennifer Lopez had contained a white powder. Buried in the powder was a Star of David charm—a symbol associated with the Jewish religion. Both Stevens and Blanco had handled the letter before it was destroyed. Investigators theorized that the mysterious powder had contained anthrax spores. They took nose swabs of all AMI employees, and the antibiotic Cipro was prescribed for those who tested positive for exposure. (A positive test for exposure does not mean that the disease will develop, but Cipro was prescribed to destroy any anthrax bacteria present in the bodies of those tested.) All employees were later advised to take an additional forty-day course of Cipro and to take advantage of an experimental anthrax vaccine program.

While investigators worked to determine the source of the AMI exposures, other anthrax cases began cropping up on the East Coast:

- **September 18, 2001. Offices of NBC News in New York City and the *New York Post* receive threatening letters containing a white powder. A trace of the letters determined that they were mailed from Trenton, New Jersey. It is likely that on this date letters laced with anthrax powder were also sent to AMI; Dan Rather, news anchor at CBS; and Peter Jennings, news anchor at ABC.**

- **The letters sent to the *New York Post* and to Tom Brokaw, news anchor at NBC, were the same. Printed in capital letters, they said:**

> 09-11-01
> THIS IS NEXT
> TAKE PENACILIN [sic] NOW
> DEATH TO AMERICA
> DEATH TO ISRAEL
> ALLAH IS GREAT

- **September 22. An editorial page assistant at the *New York Post* who opens letters to the editor notices blisters on her finger. She later tested positive for the cutaneous form of anthrax.**

- **September 26. A doctor treats a lesion on the arm of Patrick O'Donnell, a maintenance worker at the Trenton regional post office in Hamilton, New Jersey.**

- **September 27. Teresa Heller, a letter carrier at the West Trenton post office, develops a lesion on her arm.**

• **September 28.** The seven-month-old son of an **ABC** producer develops a rash and a black lesion and is hospitalized soon after his visit to the network offices. The diagnosis was at first uncertain and the baby developed a severe systemic illness. He is later diagnosed with cutaneous anthrax and given proper medical treatment. He fully recovers.

• **September 30.** Robert Stevens, the photo editor at **AMI**, starts to feel ill.

• **October 1.** Erin O'Connor, an assistant to **NBC** News anchor Tom Brokaw, sees her doctor for a low-grade fever and a rash and is prescribed the antibiotic Cipro for anthrax. Ernesto Blanco of **AMI** is hospitalized.

• **October 5.** Robert Stevens dies.

• **October 7.** The **CDC** seals the AMI building.

• **October 9.** An unknown person mails anthrax-laced letters to Senators Tom Daschle and Patrick Leahy.

• **October 12.** Letters to Senators Daschle and Leahy are misrouted and pass through a State Department mail facility in Sterling, Virginia.

• **October 15.** The letter to Senator Daschle is opened. It later tests positive for anthrax.

• **October 16.** Twelve U.S. Senate offices close. Hundreds are tested for anthrax, and exposure is confirmed for twenty-eight.

• **October 17.** House of Representatives offices close so employees can be tested. Those Senate offices that are not already closed do so two days later.

• **October 18.** Claire Fletcher, assistant to **CBS** News anchor Dan Rather, tests positive for cutaneous anthrax.

09-11-01

YOU CAN NOT STOP US.
WE HAVE THIS ANTHRAX.
YOU DIE NOW.
ARE YOU AFRAID?
DEATH TO AMERICA.
DEATH TO ISRAEL.
ALLAH IS GREAT.

TOM BROKAW
NBC TV
30 ROCKEFELLER PLAZA
NEW YORK N.Y. 10112

4TH GRADE
GREENDALE SCHOOL
FRANKLIN PARK NJ 08852

SENATOR DASCHLE
509 HART SENATE OFFICE
BUILDING
WASHINGTON D.C. 20510

TOM BROKAW, NEWS ANCHOR FOR NBC, AND SENATOR TOM DASCHLE RECEIVED ANTHRAX-LACED LETTERS IN SEPTEMBER AND OCTOBER OF 2001, RESPECTIVELY. THE RETURN ADDRESS ON THE ENVELOPE ADDRESSED TO SENATOR DASCHLE WAS THAT OF A SCHOOL IN NEW JERSEY.

IN OCTOBER 2001 THE ABOVE LETTER WAS SENT TO SENATOR TOM DASCHLE, ADDRESSED TO HIS OFFICE IN WASHINGTON, D.C. IT WAS OPENED ON OCTOBER 15.

• **October 21.** Thomas Morris Jr., fifty-five, a Washington, D.C., postal worker, dies of inhalation anthrax.

• **October 22.** Joseph Curseen, forty-seven, also a Washington postal worker, dies of inhalation anthrax. Two more postal workers are hospitalized, and nine others have symptoms of anthrax. Authorities test 2,200 postal workers.

• **October 31.** Kathy Nguyen, sixty-one, a New York City hospital worker, dies of inhalation anthrax. No one knows how she was exposed.

• **November 21.** Ottilie Lundgren, ninety-four, of Oxford, Connecticut, dies of inhalation anthrax.

It is later determined that Lundgren's exposure may have been due to contaminated mail, since she usually tore up her junk mail before throwing it away.

Anthrax spores are microscopic and paper envelopes are relatively porous, so when the postal service's mail handling equipment squeezed and otherwise manipulated the mail, the spores escaped into the air and also contaminated other pieces of mail. Mail handlers were then infected, either through inhalation of the spores or contact with contaminated mail.

The FBI continued to investigate, but as of the spring of 2003, the terrorist(s) who mailed the anthrax-laced letters had not been discovered. A major distraction during the investigation was the number of anthrax hoaxes. According to the Monterey Institute of International Studies, from 1998 to September 11, 2001, there were 400 anthrax hoaxes. From September 11, 2001 to October 2002, there were 1,500 anthrax hoaxes and a total of 1 million false alarms of all types. State and federal governments had to investigate all alarms after the 2001 attack and the cost for these investigations was $6 billion.

As Americans watched the anthrax horror progress, the federal government, infectious disease experts, and ordinary citizens feared that other biological agents that are more contagious and even more deadly than anthrax might be used against the United States. Anthrax is a serious, painful disease, but other diseases, such as smallpox, are highly contagious and would spread incredibly fast and claim many lives. (More biological weapons are discussed in Chapter 3.)

"Smallpox is a huge concern," said Dr. Peter S. Kim, executive vice president of Research and Development at Merck Pharmaceuticals in West Point, Pennsylvania, in December 2001. "It is highly contagious with a 30 percent mortality rate, and those who do survive are permanently disfigured. It's an awful disease."

Smallpox has been described as "the nightmare to end all nightmares." Those unlucky enough to be exposed to the virus experience fever, headache, and nausea for about twelve days to two weeks. Then a chickenpox-like rash appears that spreads across the body. Soon the rash hardens into blisters. About one-third of all victims die.

While there is no cure for smallpox, vaccinations can prevent it if given before exposure, or within three days of exposure. Worldwide vaccination programs were thought to have wiped out the disease in the United States by 1977 and worldwide by 1980. Vaccinations were then halted, so most Americans born since the mid-1970s have not been vaccinated.

Also in 1980, the World Health Organization (WHO) recommended that all laboratories maintaining smallpox cultures either destroy them or transfer them to one of two WHO reference laboratories, located at the Institute of Virus Preparations in Moscow, Russia, and the Centers for Disease Control and Prevention in Atlanta, Georgia. As of 2002, the United States and Russia had not destroyed their cultures. Both countries said they wanted to use them to conduct research on the virus and produce vaccine if needed in the future. Other nations were also believed to have the organism.

Fearing the worst after the 2001 anthrax attacks, the U.S. government contracted with pharmaceutical companies for enough smallpox vaccine to inoculate the entire population, in case a terrorist-induced outbreak should occur. By fall 2002 this goal had nearly been achieved. To date, however, medical experts have advised against mass inoculations for three reasons:

1. there is a one in one million chance of serious side effects, such as swelling of the brain, especially in children and those with compromised immune systems;

2. there are now more people with compromised immune systems due to AIDS, chemotherapy for cancer patients,

Could Another Anthrax Attack Occur Soon?

According to Richard F. Pilch, M.D., scientist-in-residence at the Monterey Institute's Center for Nonproliferation Studies in Monterey, California, another anthrax attack against the United States is likely to occur sometime in the next ten to twenty years. Anthrax spores can be delivered in either a wet or dry formulation. Wet formulations are made first, and these can then be used—or the process can be taken a step further—by converting a wet formulation to a dry formulation. Drying the organism is the most difficult step in the anthrax production process, says Pilch. "The person who did this [2001 attack] knew how to produce this dry formulation and do it very well." Using the biological weapons program in Iraq as an example, Pilch illustrates: "Around 1995, we knew that Iraq had anthrax spores in wet solution. They also had driers, but hadn't been able to accomplish the drying step. This is very difficult and probably won't be done by a terrorist in his garage.

"The wet anthrax spores produced by the Iraq bioweapons program could still have caused a lot of damage, but would most likely have been less effective in terms of stability, deliverability, and so on, than the dry spores used in the [2001] mail attack."

The biggest myth about chemical and biological warfare, Pilch claims, is probably that it is easy. One can learn to fly a crop duster, of course, but spreading a live organism from a plane and keeping that organism healthy enough to infect human targets on the ground can be difficult. For instance, "A crop duster attack is possible, but not easy to do. The hopper tank has to be loaded properly; the nozzle size has to be adjusted; wind, light, temperature and humidity all have to be right; it involves knowledge about flying a crop duster, and so on. Even if all of these hurdles are overcome, the shearing effect that results from forcing a biological agent through a given nozzle can kill ninety-five percent or more of that agent. Moreover, the nozzles tend to clog very easily."

Chemicals would be easier to spray from a crop duster than disease organisms, "but you couldn't spray them with pinpoint accuracy," Pilch said. (This is because chemicals are not damaged or changed by the spraying process.)

and a larger elderly population, than there were during the routine smallpox vaccinations before 1970.

3. the cost of vaccinating all Americans would be so great that such a program would use up funds needed for other medical needs.

Defending against a smallpox outbreak involves:

• informing health care givers and the general public about symptoms of the disease;

• vaccinations for health care personnel and others with early contact with victims;

• containing the spread of the disease by restricting travel and asking people to stay inside their homes.

3
The Major Biological Weapons and Their Effects

Investigators soon determined that someone who knew how to culture, handle, and disperse the bacteria had caused the anthrax infections after September 11, 2001. They knew this because:

1. The live anthrax bacteria must first be cultured in a wet medium. Then the wet medium has to be dried. During the drying process the anthrax bacteria are converted to spores. This dry formulation is converted to a fine powder capable of infecting humans. To be infective, the powder has to be fine enough to bypass the hairs in the human nose and bronchi that keep large particles from entering the respiratory tract;

2. The spores in the powder must be coated with a chemical that counteracts static electricity in order to keep them from sticking together. Otherwise, the powder forms clumps that will not disperse into the air and therefore will not be as likely to infect;

3. To safely place the anthrax powder inside envelopes, the terrorist(s) must be protected or self-infection could occur. Therefore, it is likely that the anthrax terrorist had access to specialized equipment that allows one to handle dangerous materials with gloves, through a barrier, thus reducing personal danger of exposure;

4. The paper letters were folded in a way that ensured the spores would stay inside the envelopes until the letters were opened and unfolded. (Unfortunately, this was not the case. Apparently the terrorist(s) did not know that the spores were small enough to pass through the pores in the paper when the letters were subjected to postal equipment manipulation.)

5. The letters specifically targeted news media personalities and politicians in the Democratic party, instead of random members of the population. (However, since the letters contaminated postal facilities, the AMI building, Senate and House offices, and other pieces of mail, the infections were not confined to the letter recipients.)

For all of these reasons, it was apparent that someone had the ability to grow or steal anthrax cultures, induce the bacteria to produce spores, make a fine powder from the bacteria spores, and safely insert the anthrax powder into paper envelopes. They also had the malice and disregard for human life to use the disease-laden powder as a weapon.

Some of the characteristics that make certain organisms more suitable than others for use as bioweapons are:

- **they can cause serious illness or death;**

- **they are highly contagious, so that one infected person can spread the disease to many others;**

- **because they would infect many people, they would strain hospital resources;**

- **diseases, such as smallpox and Ebola, cause terrible symptoms that are alarming to the public;**

- **cultures can be purchased or stolen and then manufactured on a large scale;**

- **the organism can be converted to a form that is readily dispersed in the air or in water and food supplies;**

- **they are highly resilient and have a long shelf life;**

- **there is a short incubation period between infection and the onset of symptoms;**

- **they resist medical treatment; and**

- **the attacking force can be protected against the disease agent.**

Since all pathogens do not share these characteristics, a limited number—an estimated thirty in all—have been used

WORKERS IN AFRICA EVACUATE A VICTIM OF THE EBOLA VIRUS.

in experiments to develop biological weapons. The anthrax bacterium meets most of the above criteria. The exceptions are that it is not highly contagious and is treatable with certain antibiotics.

Viruses may be preferred by bioterrorists over bacteria, because most are highly contagious and difficult or impossible to treat medically. They are also much smaller than bacteria, and therefore more likely than bacteria to be inhaled by victims. In *Germs: Biological Weapons and America's Secret War*, Judith Miller, Stephen Engelberg, and William Broad illustrate the difference in size of the two organisms by comparing cars and minivans, representing bacteria, to cell phones (viruses). "Viruses are small because they lack most of life's usual parts and processes," they add, "such as metabolism and respiration. Scientists consider them barely alive, seeing them more as robots than organisms. To thrive and reproduce, they invade a cell and take over its biochemical gear, often at the expense of the host." Their small size allows them to slip into cells, where they are often undetected by the body's immune system until they have begun to cause damage.

One effective defense against some viruses and bacteria is vaccination. The vaccination process varies. In some cases, a small amount of live pathogen (disease organism) is introduced into a person's body. In other cases, a weakened pathogen, a dead pathogen, or a similar but less deadly pathogen is introduced into a person's body, either orally, or by injection, or through the skin. The vaccine acts as an antigen, or foreign substance in the body. The body's immune system responds to the foreign invader by producing antibodies against the disease organism. Antibodies are proteins produced by the body. They attack the foreign substance introduced by a vaccine, and thus protect the vaccinated individual against a specific disease.

The antibodies remain in the bloodstream, along with many other antigen-specific antibodies developed over the years, to protect against disease.

It takes time, however, for antibodies to develop and do their work, so individuals must be vaccinated before a bioterrorism attack or soon after exposure, in some cases, in order for vaccination to work as a defense. In warfare or acts of terrorism, the group using bioweapons can, in many cases, inoculate their own troops or individuals against the pathogen, thus ensuring their safety. (Except in cases where there is no vaccine for the organism being used.)

The Centers for Disease Control and Prevention has identified five pathogens and one bacterial toxin as most likely to be used as biological weapons. These include the disease organisms for smallpox, anthrax, bubonic and pneumonic plague, tularemia, and the viral hemorrhagic fevers, and the botulinum toxin. Several more agents are considered to have potential for use as biological weapons but are either less effective or more difficult to prepare for dispersal.

AGENTS THAT REPRESENT THE HIGHEST RISK TO NATIONAL AND WORLD SECURITY:

Smallpox
Disease-Causing Organism: variola major (virus)

Effects. The incubation period for smallpox is approximately twelve days. The disease is not contagious until symptoms appear, after which it becomes highly contagious. Each time a smallpox victim breathes, he or she releases more virus particles into the air, where they enter the respiratory tracts of others and cause new infections. Smallpox begins with a red rash, low fever, fatigue, headache, and nausea. The rash appears on the face and torso first, then spreads to the arms and legs. The flat red lesions soon turn into pocks—hardened, pus-filled blisters. This phase of the disease is extremely painful—some who have had smallpox say it resembles the agony of having a bad skin burn. Victims may also experience severe abdominal pain and delirium. Scabs finally form over the blisters and then drop off, leaving pitted scars where the pocks were embedded in the skin. Thirty percent of victims of the most deadly form of smallpox die, probably from a breakdown of the immune system.

Treatment. There is no cure for smallpox. Antiviral drugs are being developed that may help to shorten and moderate the course of infection, but to date, supportive therapy—intravenous fluids, drugs to control fever or pain, and antibiotics for secondary infections—is the only treatment available.

Prevention. Vaccination can prevent smallpox from developing if given before exposure, and is effective even after exposure to the disease if given within three days. Vaccine has been in short supply, but in 2002 the federal government announced plans to purchase 300 million doses of the vaccine, enough for everyone in the United States. Routine vaccination for smallpox ended in the mid-1970s, when scientists declared that the disease had been eradicated. People who were vaccinated before that time may not have full protection against the disease, because the inoculations are effective for only about ten years. The vaccine against smallpox does not contain the smallpox virus. Instead, it contains another live virus called vaccinia, which is a pox-like virus related to smallpox.

The vaccine cannot cause smallpox, but an estimated one-third of all vaccinated individuals have mild symptoms that may cause them to miss work or school for a

short time. For every 1 million people vaccinated, it is estimated that the following side effects would occur:

- **one or two deaths;**

- **fourteen to fifty-two people would have a potentially
  life-threatening reaction, such as:**

    o **inflammation of the brain (encephalitis),**

    o **progressive vaccinia, an infection that destroys skin,**

    o **eczema vaccinatum, skin rashes caused by
      infections such as eczema;**

- **approximately 1,000 people would have serious but
  not life-threatening reactions, such as a toxic or allergic reaction at the vaccination site and the spreading
  of the vaccinia virus to other parts of the body and to
  other people.**

Because of the potential for side effects, individuals
who should not be vaccinated are those: under one year of
age; those with weakened immune systems; those with
eczema and other skin conditions; those with burns that
have not healed; those who are allergic to the vaccine; those
who are ill; and those who use steroid drops in their eyes.

If the smallpox virus were actually to be released into
the population, control of the resulting epidemic would de-
pend upon early detection, isolation of infected individuals, tracking contacts of all infected victims, and a massive
vaccination program.

Anthrax

Disease-Causing Organism: *Bacillus anthracis (bacteria)*

Effects. The effects of infection by anthrax bacteria were discussed at length in Chapter 2. In short, the cutaneous form of anthrax appears as a fever and a red rash that develops into black lesions. Symptoms of the gastrointestinal form of the disease include fever, nausea, abdominal pain, diarrhea, bloody stools, and vomitus (material ejected from the stomach by vomiting). Those who develop inhalation anthrax commonly experience fever, shortness of breath, cough, nausea, fatigue, headache, sweats, and chest pain. All forms of the disease can be fatal without treatment.

Treatment. Antibiotics that are usually effective against anthrax include penicillin, Doxycycline and Ciprofloxacin (Cipro).

Prevention. There is a vaccine for anthrax, but to be effective it must be given before symptoms of the disease appear. To date, six inoculations over a period of eighteen months are required to provide complete protection. In normal times the military and personnel who work with animals in occupations where they could come in contact with anthrax are the only people who are vaccinated. Because of the number of inoculations required, the general public is not vaccinated.

Bubonic and Pneumonic Plague

Disease-Causing Organism: *Yersinia pestis (bacteria)*

Effects. Infected fleas spread the disease when they bite mammals, including humans. Since rats, chipmunks, prairie dogs, and other rodents harbor fleas, and poor living conditions and sanitary habits give rise to large rodent populations, the disease spread rapidly before the twentieth century, and it still occurs in various parts of the world, including the United States. After infected fleas bite people, chills and fever set in within one to eight days. Six to eight hours after the first symptoms appear, painful lumps form under the surface of the skin. These are the "buboes" that give the bubonic plague its name. Lymph nodes swell, particularly in the neck, groin, and armpits, and become extremely painful. Antibiotics can effectively treat this form of the disease if treatment is begun early. If an infected person receives no medical treatment, the lumps grow in size and darken as tissues are infected.

The disease-causing agent can also be spread from one individual to another through the air. Inhalation of the bacteria causes pneumonic plague, an especially deadly form of the disease. Within one to six days after inhaling the organism, an infected person develops severe pneumonia. The lungs fill with fluid, cutting off the oxygen supply to other organs. As the plague organisms are attacked by the body's immune system, they are stimulated to produce a potent toxin that eventually causes the collapse of the circulatory system. Convulsions, disorientation, coma and death follow, usually within eighteen hours.

Treatment. Plague can be treated with the antibiotics streptomycin, tetracycline, gentamicin, and Doxycycline.

Prevention. Improvements in cities' sanitation and public health systems have helped to get rid of rats and other pests that harbor fleas that carry the plague organism. However, 2,000 cases of plague are reported throughout the world each year, and the disease has also surfaced in the southwestern United States, where prairie dogs and chipmunks carry it.

An effective vaccine against bubonic plague has been developed, but booster shots must be given every six months, and there is no vaccine against pneumonic plague.

Tularemia

Disease-Causing Organism: *Francisella tularensis (bacteria)*

Effects. Tularemia-causing bacteria live naturally in rabbits and other rodents. Hunters and people who process rabbit fur have long been aware of "rabbit fever" caused by the bacteria. People can also contract the disease from the bite of infected North American ticks. There are two types of naturally occurring tularemia. One is more common in the United States than in other countries and can be fatal 60 percent of the time if left untreated. The second type is usually not fatal. It is found more often in European countries, particularly Scandinavia.

The tularemia organism does not form spores, but can survive for weeks at low temperatures in water, wet soil, hay, straw, or decaying animal carcasses. The most virulent form of tularemia is the inhaled or typhoidal variety, which can cause disease after inhalation of only ten organisms. Tularemia is rarely spread from person to person. Within three to five days, a person exposed to the *Francisella tularensis* bacteria will develop chills, fever, headache, general weakness, chest pain, cough, and will undergo weight loss. Symptoms soon progress to pneumonia, and, without treatment, to respiratory failure, shock, and death.

Treatment. The antibiotics streptomycin and tetracycline are used to treat tularemia.

Prevention. In the United States, laboratory workers have been given a vaccine against tularemia, but protection against inhalation tularemia is incomplete.

Viral Hemorrhagic Fevers (VHFs)

Disease-Causing Organisms: Hemorrhagic fevers are caused by a variety of viruses. The causative organism is in parentheses for each of the following diseases: Ebola and Marburg fevers (*Filoviridae*), Lassa fever (*Arenaviridae*), Congo-Crimean hemorrhagic fever (*Nairovirus*), Hantavirus

47

(*Bunyaviridae*), Rift Valley fever (*Phlebovirus*), and Yellow fever and Dengue hemorrhagic fever (*Flaviviridae*).

Effects. The VHF group causes painful diseases that weaken blood vessels in victims and cause body fluids to leak from tissues and orifices. All except Dengue fever are transmitted via the air or by contaminated objects. Symptoms are the same for most VHFs, and include fever, rashes, body aches, headaches, fatigue, and, in advanced cases, hemorrhage from many areas of the body. Fatality rates among the infected range from 60 to 90 or even 100 percent. Because the organism almost always kills its host, the spread of the disease is limited. (When all hosts have died, spread of the disease slows and eventually stops.)

Treatment. Presently there are no antiviral drugs to treat any of the VHF diseases.

Prevention: Spread of the disease may be slowed if workers caring for patients use strict protective measures, such as hand washing, wearing double-thickness gloves, heavy gowns, leg and shoe coverings, face shields or goggles, and masks or air-purifying respirators. A vaccine exists only for yellow fever.

Some organisms are deadly because they produce toxins that act as poisons in the body. These agents include mycotoxins produced by fungi (the substance present in the "Yellow Rain" observed in the Vietnam War), the fungi themselves (often used to destroy crops), and toxins produced by staphylococcus bacteria, the castor bean (ricin), Japanese puffer fish and red tide organisms (saxitoxin), and botulineum bacteria.

Botulinum Toxin

Disease-Causing Organism: *Clostridium botulinum* (bacteria)

Effects. The organism that causes the condition called botulism normally lives in soil and in the intestinal tracts of domesticated animals. It thrives in meat and other nonacid foods that have been improperly canned. The toxin produced by *Clostridium botulinum* acts on the nervous system, and a tiny amount can produce symptoms. Within twenty-four to thirty-six hours after exposure to botulism toxin, victims experience fatigue, weakness, dizziness, headache, nausea, vomiting, diarrhea, and abdominal pain. Blurred vision and difficulty in swallowing and speaking may also occur. As symptoms progress, the muscles used in respiration are paralyzed, and death occurs.

Treatment. Antitoxins are available and will stop the progression of symptoms if given early enough. Advanced cases also require respirators to take over breathing functions for paralyzed muscles. The antitoxin for advanced cases is available only from the Centers for Disease Control and Prevention via state and local health departments.

Prevention. In normal conditions, boiling canned food for ten minutes at 212 degrees Fahrenheit (100 °C) destroys the toxin. Laboratory workers have been given an experimental antitoxin to prevent the development of botulism if they are exposed to the poisonous bacterial toxin. However, the antitoxin provides immunity for several months only, and supplies are limited.

Ricin and Saxitoxin

Lethal Element: Ricin is a deadly poison derived from the castor plant (*Ricinus communis*). While ricin is not a living organism, it enters human cells much like a virus, where it disrupts protein production. Ricin is similar in its effects to saxitoxin, a poison found in Japanese puffer fish and the organisms that cause red tides. Saxitoxin is a neurotoxin (affects the nervous system) that can also be chemically manufactured in small quantities.

Treatment. The United States continues to work on possible vaccines and antidotes for these poisons.

Other bacteria and viruses have been studied for suitability as bioweapons, including those that cause Q fever, brucellosis, glanders, melsosdosis, viral encephalitis, psittacosis, and salmonella. Q fever is caused by the rickettsiae (organisms that are between bacteria and viruses in size) *Coxiella burnetii.* Cattle raisers and slaughterhouse workers are among those most likely to be infected naturally. Q fever is seldom fatal, and most people fully recover. Brucellosis and glanders are diseases that mainly infect cattle, sheep, horses and mules, but they can be spread to humans and in some cases can be fatal.

In one of the most serious acts of bioterrorism ever carried out on American soil, none of the organisms or toxins listed above was used. In 1984, a religious cult based in Wasco County, near The Dalles, Oregon, used the common salmonella bacteria to poison hundreds of local citizens. The cult was composed of followers of Bhagwan Shree Rajneesh. The group was first based in Poona, India, but then moved to Wasco County, Oregon, after Rajneesh purchased a 64,000-acre ranch there. The Rajneeshees, as cult members were called, dressed only in shades of red, grew their own food, and had their own medical center. In just three years, the 4,000-member group built a small city on the vast uninhabited ranchland.

At first, most of the local residents of nearby communities The Dalles and Antelope welcomed the cult members. But then the group managed to take over Antelope's town council and renamed the town Rajneesh. They also took over the local school and turned what had previously been a combination gas station, store, and restaurant into a health-food café. They formed their own police force that often harassed and mistreated local citizens. Then the Rajneeshees decided to take over the Wasco County commission. They moved in 3,000 homeless people from New York and other cities to vote for Rajneeshee candidates for county commissioner. Local residents resisted by vowing not to vote for Rajneeshee candidates and by campaigning against them.

As the campaigns for county commissioner heated up, people in The Dalles began to fall ill at an alarming rate. They suffered from stomach cramps, chills, fever, dizziness and disorientation, nausea and vomiting, and severe diarrhea. Victims, most of whom had eaten recently at local restaurants' salad bars, were left weak and dehydrated. A pathologist identified the organism causing the sickness as salmonella poisoning, caused by *Salmonella typhimurium* bacteria. A deliberate act of bioterrorism was suspected, but local authorities had no proof that the Rajneeshees were guilty.

The Rajneeshees lost the election, despite having registered thousands of homeless people to vote. More than a

BHAGWAN SHREE RAJNEESH (IN THE WHITE ROBE) WITH HIS FOLLOWERS ON THEIR COMPOUND IN WASCO COUNTY, OREGON, IN 1985.

year later when a few cult members confessed, Oregonians learned that the Rajneeshees had poisoned at least 751 local people during the fall of 1984. Cult members had sprinkled their disease-bearing cocktail on local salad bars and had stirred it into salad dressings and coffee cream containers. They had hoped to make the local voters too sick to vote, thus ensuring victory for the Rajneeshee candidates.

In 1985 the Bhagwan Rajneesh was on his way out of the United States when he was arrested in Charlotte, North Carolina. Two of his co-leaders, known as Ma Anand Sheela and Ma Anand Puja (Diane Ivonne Onang), were arrested in Germany, where they had fled to escape arrest. They were extradited to the United States. There were no anti-terrorism laws at the time, so the Bhagwan was charged with violating immigration laws and a federal consumer-product tampering law. His two co-leaders, who had actually spearheaded the salmonella poisoning operation, were charged with attempted murder, and with causing the salmonella outbreak in The Dalles, in addition to other crimes.

Sheela and Puja were each sentenced to twenty-five years in prison and fined several thousand dollars. Through shrewd legal tactics, however, they served just four years in a California jail, were released early for good behavior, and then quickly moved to Europe.

The Bhagwan received a ten-year suspended prison sentence and paid $400,000 in fines. He left the United States for good. He died of heart failure, in Parma, India, on January 19, 1990. He was fifty-eight years old.

There were no deaths from the salmonella poisonings, but there could have been, since the very young, the elderly, and those with existing medical conditions are most susceptible to the bacteria. Most of the restaurants where the tainted salad bars were found did not recover financially and were forced to close, even though their owners had played no part in the bioterror attacks.

Why have rogue nations (those who do not follow the rules of the international community), fanatical political or religious groups, or, sometimes, deranged individuals felt the need to develop biological weapons or to use those they have bought or stolen? Although these weapons are used to frighten people, those who want to use them also know that they are:

- **less expensive than nuclear weapons and easier to produce;**

- **hard to detect, at first, when released in a population;**

- **effective in eliminating or disabling large numbers of people;**

- **difficult to trace to a source.**

In addition, unlike bombs and gunfire, biological weapons strike silently. People are unaware that they have been attacked until symptoms of disease develop, and by that time, over-stressed health systems and fear have made a population vulnerable.

4
The Major Chemical Weapons and Their Effects

The nation or organization that uses disease-causing organisms as weapons is probably also prepared to use chemicals if they are available. Chemical weapons are less difficult to develop because one does not have the problem of keeping an organism alive. Developing effective biological weapons requires some knowledge of microbiology, but chemical weapons can be produced by anyone with a basic knowledge of chemistry. Chemical weapons are effective as instruments of terror, but unlike biological weapons, they do not hurt or kill anyone who was not originally exposed.

Like biological weapons, chemical weapons may be chosen because they kill humans, animals, and plants cheaply, silently, and without destroying buildings or property. The cost of killing people with chemical weapons has been estimated at about $600 per square kilometer (.62 miles) compared to $2,000 per square kilometer using conventional weapons.

Lethal chemicals are also easier to disperse than biological weapons. They can be sprayed from crop dusting planes or from trucks, from fire extinguishers and other aerosol canisters, or they can be placed in water supplies. They are easier to disperse from crop dusters or other sprayers than most biological weapons, because the mechanism does not have to be adapted to keep an organism alive. And chemicals are usually not immediately affected by sunlight, humidity, temperature and other environmental conditions, as are biological organisms.

The most infamous example of the use of chemical weapons in modern times is probably the 1995 gassing of passengers on the Tokyo subway by members of Aum Shinrikyo, a fanatical religious cult based in Japan. The 20,000 to 40,000 members of the cult believed that the new millennium would bring nuclear war. Apparently, they also believed that the best defense against such a war was to strike first, against an enemy who was sketchily defined.

On March 20, 1995, many Tokyo workers on their way to jobs, and other passengers riding in five separate subway cars during the morning rush hour, suddenly felt nauseous. Their noses then began to run, their chests felt tight, and they had difficulty seeing. Soon, the affected passengers were suffering cramps, headache, and vomiting. Some twitched, jerked, and staggered as they tried to walk. By the time the subway trains were stopped and emergency medical personnel arrived, some passengers had lost bowel and bladder control. Others were convulsing or unconscious. A few had already died.

Law enforcement officials had been watching Aum cult members for some time, and they soon determined that Aum operatives had boarded the subway trains carrying plastic bags filled with the deadly nerve agent sarin. At an agreed-upon time, they used umbrella tips to poke holes in the plastic bags. As the sarin was released, it spilled on the floor and began to evaporate, forming a deadly gas that the innocent subway passengers inhaled.

While the Aum's method of delivering the sarin was crude, it was effective. Twelve people who rode the subway that morning in March were killed, and 3,800 were injured. Of those who were injured, 1,000 were hospitalized. Those who did not die from exposure to the gas were seriously ill. Only the inept preparation of the sarin had prevented many more casualties. Since the Aum cult was under close surveillance by the authorities, their sarin supply was

ON MARCH 20, 1995, MEMBERS OF AUM SHINRIKYO IN JAPAN, RELEASED SARIN GAS IN THE TOKYO SUBWAY. TWELVE PASSENGERS WERE KILLED, AND 3,800 WERE INJURED. OF THOSE WHO WERE INJURED, 1,000 WERE HOSPITALIZED. THOSE WHO DID NOT DIE FROM EXPOSURE TO THE GAS WERE SERIOUSLY ILL. HERE, UNINJURED PASSENGERS HELP THOSE WHO WERE EXPOSED TO THE GAS.

low. To stretch the supply for the subway attack, they mixed the sarin with a solvent, thus greatly reducing the toxicity of the chemical weapon.

Authorities were alerted to the Aum cult's terrorist activities in 1994 when the sect rigged a refrigerated truck to spray sarin throughout the neighborhood where several magistrates (judges) who were about to rule against them in a legal matter lived. The judges were injured, but none died. However, seven bystanders were killed and 500 others were taken to local hospitals. Approximately 200 of the injured required at least one night of hospitalization.

The Aum group had tried to use biological weapons even before the 1995 subway attack. In nine separate attempts, cult members sprayed botulinum toxin near the Japanese Diet, the Imperial Palace, two American naval bases, and several other locations. None of the attacks were successful—no one became ill or died. Aum operatives had also attempted to use anthrax, but were unsuccessful because the strain they used was harmless. Unfortunately, the cult was more successful with chemical weapons.

After the subway attack, more than 200 Aum cult members were arrested, including the cult's leader, Shoko Asahara. (His real name was Chizuo Matsumoto.) By 2002, some 120 cult members were still in jail, or had been convicted of crimes related to the subway attack and the earlier attack that had sickened three judges and killed seven bystanders.

Asahara's trial began in 1996 and was still in progress in September 2002. The trial moved slowly because of the complicated Japanese legal system, and because the defendant refused to cooperate with the prosecution. Many of the arrested cult members were sentenced to prison terms, and some operatives were sentenced to hang. The cult's legal status as a church was revoked. While some of its assets were confiscated, others remained unaccounted for. The Japanese government considered passing a law to disband the cult, but probably to avoid the appearance of persecution, they did not. As of the fall of 2002, the cult was reassembling in Japan under a new name, "Aleph," from the first letter of the Hebrew alphabet, signifying a new beginning. The group had fewer members than before the 1995 subway attack, but was actively recruiting.

The sarin used by the Aums is a nerve agent. There are seven major categories of chemical warfare agents. They are classified according to their primary effects on the human body:

1. choking gases (lung irritants)
2. blister agents or vesicants (mustard gas)
3. blood agents
4. nerve agents (sarin, tabun, soman, VX)
5. incapacitants
6. harassing or riot-control agents
7. vomiting agents

The following chemicals are nerve agents or toxic organophosporus compounds. Most were developed from pesticides. They affect the human nervous system and pose the most immediate threat as weapons:

Sarin

Chemical Name: Isopropyl methyl phosphonofluoridate

Characteristics. Sarin is a colorless liquid that does not give off an odor when vaporized. Sarin vapor is also colorless. It evaporates quickly and can be made to last longer in an area through the addition of certain oils or petroleum products.

Effects. Sarin is a nerve agent that acts on the nervous system when inhaled as a gas or absorbed through the skin in liquid form. Victims of exposure to the chemical at first notice a runny nose, constriction of the pupils, and tightness in the chest. As symptoms progress, victims have difficulty breathing, become nauseous, and lose control of bladder and bowel functions. At this stage victims also twitch and jerk and soon become comatose. Death by suffocation follows as muscles that control breathing go into spasm.

Comments. Sarin was developed in Germany in 1938. Its name was derived from the first initials of the chemists who created it.

Tabun

Chemical Name: Ethyl N, N-dimethyl phosphoramido-cyanidate

Characteristics. Tabun is an amber-colored, nearly odorless chemical that vaporizes into a colorless poisonous gas.

Effects. Tabun is a nerve agent that acts on the human body much the same as sarin. In liquid form, tabun is absorbed through the skin, but it is just as poisonous if inhaled as a gas. Death can occur instantly or within twenty minutes, depending upon the dose. If a lethal dose is not received and medical treatment is not immediately available, permanent damage to the nervous system may occur.

Comments. Tabun was developed in Germany in 1937, as a result of a scientist's work on pesticides. The first time one of the nerve agents was used in war was during the Iran-Iraq war of 1980 to 1988, when Iraq repeatedly used tabun. Its name has no known significance.

Soman

Chemical Name: Pinacolyl methyl phosphonofluoridate

Characteristics. Soman is a colorless liquid. It vaporizes into a colorless gas that smells like rotting fruit. It is twice as lethal as sarin and can remain in an area for a day or longer, depending on environmental conditions.

Effects. Since soman is also a nerve agent, it causes the same symptoms as sarin and tabun, resulting in death in about fifteen minutes if a lethal dose is absorbed through the skin or eyes, or inhaled.

Comments. Soman was also developed in Germany during World War II. The Soviets allegedly stockpiled the chemical during the Cold War.

VX

Chemical Name: O-ethyl S-(2-diisopropylaminoethyl) methylphosphonothioate

Characteristics. VX was developed in Porton Down, Wiltshire, England, in 1952. Great Britain traded VX technology to the United States in exchange for information on thermonuclear weapons. In liquid form VX is usually colorless. It is odorless as a gas. Its oily properties make it stick to skin and other surfaces, where it is often difficult to remove. VX is more toxic than any of the other nerve agents listed above. A tiny amount of the chemical can kill a person.

Effects. Like other nerve agents, VX acts by disabling the nervous system. Symptoms of exposure are the same as those listed above for the other nerve agents. After exposure, death occurs in minutes. Atropine and other chemicals are given upon VX exposure. The skin must be decontaminated immediately, as well. Military personnel in danger of exposure to VX carry a skin decontamination kit containing pre-treated wipes and a decontamination powder that is mixed with water and applied to the skin.

Comments. The name "VX" is said to stand for "extremely virulent."

Mustard Gas

Chemical Name: 1,1-thiobis (2-chloroethane)

Characteristics. Mustard gas is a manufactured chemical that contains sulfur mustard. The chemical does not behave as a gas under normal conditions. Mustard gas is not actually a gas but a colorless and odorless liquid. When mixed with other chemicals it is brown and smells like garlic. Mustard gas does not occur in nature and can enter the environment only through evaporation from water and soil or through accidental release by people. It breaks down quickly when exposed to the air or when it enters animal tissues.

Effects. Mustard gas is a vesicant, which means that it causes skin burns and blisters. It can also damage the respiratory tract. People exposed to mustard gas experience

IN 1988, DURING THE IRAN-IRAQ WAR, IRAQ'S DICTATOR, SADDAM HUSSEIN, ORDERED THE USE OF SARIN, MUSTARD GAS, AND CYANIDE ON KURDS LIVING IN NORTHERN IRAQ WHO WERE SUSPECTED OF SIDING WITH IRAN. THE ATTACK KILLED 4,000 CIVILIANS.

burning eyes, swelling eyelids, increased eye blinking, and difficulty breathing. If victims survive exposure, they may have long-term respiratory system damage.

Comments. Mustard gas was used extensively in World War I, and it was reportedly used in the Iran-Iraq war from 1980 to 1988. The United States no longer makes or stockpiles mustard gas.

Listed above are those chemical warfare agents that are most likely to be used by terrorists or the military because they are the most lethal or debilitating. Other chemical agents are just as injurious, and also cause death when used in large concentrations. For example, among the choking gases that have been used in warfare are chlorine (the substance that burns your eyes in a swimming pool) and phosgene. Both of these chemicals, when used as weapons, are delivered as a gas. They cause eye irritation, respiratory distress and, in large enough doses, can cause death.

Blood agents are poisons that block the body's oxygen utilization system, causing asphyxiation. Germany used the blood agent hydrogen cyanide during World War II in its infamous gas chambers to kill prisoners of war and other groups. Japanese forces also used hydrocyanic acid grenades in World War II. Other blood agents used as weapons include the cyanogens, chlorides, arsine, and carbon monoxide.

Incapacitants are chemical warfare agents that can disorient, paralyze, or otherwise render enemy troops and civilians helpless. These chemicals include belladonna, ergot, and lysergic acid diethylamide (LSD). Incapacitants usually have the following properties:

- **their effects last hours or even days;**
- **but do not cause death or lasting injury;**
- **recovery seldom requires medical treatment;**
- **they are easy to deliver, potent, and easily stored; and**
- **many of them cause hallucinations.**

Other less deadly chemical agents have been used to harass the enemy during wartime and to control riots in peacetime. Law enforcement officers frequently use tear gas to control riots. Tear gas irritates the eyes and burns the skin, but its effects wear off relatively fast, and it does not usually cause lasting injury.

Military forces have used herbicides and vomiting agents to harass or incapacitate the enemy. For example, the herbicide Agent Orange was widely used in the Vietnam War to destroy plants that provided cover for the enemy and to kill food crops used by the enemy. Agent Orange contains varying amounts of dioxin, a chemical existing in nature that is harmful to all living organisms and is especially harmful in concentrated dosages. Exposure to Agent Orange has been linked with chemical acne (a skin condition where pimples and pustules form), and some forms of cancer, including non-Hodgkin's lymphoma, Hodgkin's disease, and soft-tissue sarcoma.

Vomiting agents include many arsenic-based compounds, such as diphenylchlorarsine and diphenylcyanarsine. In addition to nausea and vomiting, these chemicals cause pain to the eyes, nose, and throat. In closed areas, vomiting agents can kill.

"Fondly do we hope,
Fervently do we pray,
That this mighty scourge of war
"May speedily pass away. . ."
Abraham Lincoln (1809–1865)

5

History and Uses of Chemical and Biological Weapons

Chemical and biological weapons are not new. As soon as people discovered that smoke made others choke and could fend off an attack, they probably began thinking about how to use toxic smoke to their advantage in combat. It may have taken a bit longer for people to notice that when one person was ill, others nearby soon fell ill, too, but once realization dawned, it was a short step to the use of biological weapons.

The Greek historian Thucydides reported the first recorded use of poison gas during the Peloponnesian War between Athens and Sparta (431–404 B.C.E.), when flaming pitch and sulfur mixtures were used to produce toxic smoke. The Spartan armies were also said to have used vapor clouds of arsenic against the enemy. During the fourth century B.C.E., the Chinese used toxic smoke to poison enemy mine workers. Early armies also threw burning oil and fireballs on attacking troops.

In the Middle Ages, before the invention of gunpowder, a flammable mixture known as Greek fire was used as a weapon. Greek fire was probably a mixture of sulfur, naphtha, quicklime, resin, pitch, and saltpeter. It was an excellent weapon against ships of the time, because it floated on water and easily set fire to the wooden ships. Not only did the ships burn, the vapors from the fire suffocated sailors in the vicinity. The Byzantines, from the eastern portion of the Roman Empire, loaded bronze tubes with the mixture and then mounted the tubes on the prows of their ships and on the walls around Constantinople. When the mixture in the tubes was ignited, jets of liquid fire were aimed at enemy ships. In 678 and again in 717 the Byzantines destroyed two Saracen fleets with Greek fire. These fire-shooting tubes were the precursors of modern day flamethrowers.

Attempts to use biological weapons also date far back in time:

• **In the sixth century B.C.E., the Assyrians reportedly poisoned enemy wells with rye ergot, a poisonous mold that causes hallucinations.**

• **Roman armies dumped dead animals in enemies' water supplies, hoping to spread sickness and panic.**

• **Two thousand years ago, Scythian soldiers dipped their arrowheads in manure and rotting corpses to add killing power to their weapons. (Scythians lived in ancient Eurasia, an area bounded by the Danube on the west and the borders of China on the east.)**

THIS FIFTEENTH CENTURY WORK OF ART, LOCATED IN TOURNAI, FRANCE, DEPICTS THE BURIAL OF VICTIMS OF BUBONIC PLAGUE—ALSO CALLED THE BLACK DEATH.

• Hannibal, in preparing for a naval battle against King Eumenes of Pergamum in 184 B.C.E., ordered that pots filled with poisonous snakes be thrown onto the decks of enemy ships—a crude but effective form of biological warfare.

• In medieval times, the Tartars catapulted plague-infected corpses into the city of Kaffa in the Russian Crimea, thus spreading the disease among the enemy. Bubonic plague—also called the Black Death—wiped out about a third of Europe's population between 1347 and 1351, and is said to have started in and around Kaffa.

"Gassed"

"Gas! GAS! Quick, boys!—An ecstasy of fumbling,
"Fitting the clumsy helmets just in time;
"But someone still was yelling out and stumbling
"And flound'ring like a man in fire or lime . . .
"Dim, through the misty panes and thick green light,
"As under a green sea, I saw him drowning.
"In all my dreams, before my helpless sight,
"He plunges at me guttering, choking, drowning. . . . "

That poem was written by Lieutenant Wilfred Owen of the Royal Army, who was killed in action during World War I in France on November 4, 1918. This excerpt is from *Owen's Dulce et Decorum Est* published in *The Collected Poems of Wilfred Owen*, Chatto & Windus, Ltd.,1963.

THE PAINTING "GASSED" BY JOHN SINGER SARGENT, ON DISPLAY AT THE IMPERIAL WAR MUSEUM IN GREAT BRITAIN, DEPICTS WORLD WAR I SOLDIERS ON THE BATTLEFIELD. MANY ARE SUFFERING FROM EYE INJURIES AS A RESULT OF EXPOSURE TO MUSTARD OR CHLORINE GAS.

• **In the sixteenth century, Francisco Pizarro, a Spanish conquistador, gave South American Incas smallpox-contaminated clothing. English military leaders in the French and Indian Wars (1754–1763) used the same tactic to spread smallpox among Native Americans by giving them virus-infected blankets. This was thought to have led to the loss of Fort Carillon to the English when the Native Americans defending the fort fell ill.**

The extensive use of chemical weapons and, to some extent, biological weapons began in the twentieth century. For instance, there was evidence that during World War I (fought between the Central Powers—Germany, Austria-Hungary and what is now Turkey—and the Allies—Great Britain, France, Russia, Italy, and the United States), German agents deliberately infected horses and cattle in the United States that were to be shipped to France with glanders, a bacterial disease of donkeys, mules, and horses that can spread to humans. Glanders in humans produces systemic blood infections, severe lung infections, and inflammation of the skin and eyes. Without antibiotic treatment, victims often die from the disease. The Germans may also have infected horses and donkeys used by Tsarist troops in World War I, thus hindering Russia's ability to send artillery to the Eastern Front.

German scientists had made great strides in chemistry in the years prior to World War I, so Germany was well prepared to use chemical weapons when the war began and, in fact, was the first to do so. During World War I, on April 22, 1915, the Germans released some 160 tons (145 metric tons) of chlorine gas over Allied troops near Ypres, Belgium. The large amount of gas released killed 5,000 men. Another attack two days later killed 500 Allied soldiers. A total of 15,000 men were injured in the attacks.

Those who survived the attacks experienced permanent respiratory and eye injuries.

Many other chemical weapons were developed and used during World War I. In addition to using chlorine gas, British, American, and German forces used mustard gas and phosgene gas on enemy troops. (Phosgene or carbonyl dichloride is odorless and similar to chlorine in its effects. It usually kills victims within twenty-four hours after exposure by destroying tissue in the lungs.) The chemical weapons were delivered in artillery shells or in canisters. A total of about 113,000 tons (102,512 metric tons) of chemicals were used as weapons in World War I, killing 92,000 people and injuring many thousands more. Phosgene alone was said to have been responsible for 80 percent of the soldiers killed by chemicals in World War I.

So frightening was the prospect of being gassed that soldiers fighting in World War I often developed a psychological condition called "gas fright." Just the fear of being poisoned, or the belief that gas had been used nearby could cause soldiers to report to aid stations, sometimes with stomachaches, burning eyes, and disorientation, even though there had been no exposure to gas. As stated in a 1918 U.S. Army report:

> One form of psychoneurosis, "Gas Fright," was very common but most cases could be restored to the lines after a few hours' rest. One instance occurred where an entire platoon of machine gunners developed this form of psychosis. These men were eating their meal just before dark when a shell fell and burst at a distance of about 100 meters [328 feet]. They continued eating and many of them had finished when someone yelled Gas! and said their food had been gassed. All the men were seized with

gas fright and a few minutes later made their way to the Aid Station. To an inexperienced eye they could have easily been diagnosed as gassed patients. They came in a stooping posture, holding their abdomens and complaining of pains in the stomach, while their faces bore anxious, frightened expressions and some had even vomited. After reassurance, treatment with tablets of sodium bicarbonate, and a night's rest, they were quite well again.

Chemical Casualties in World War I

Country	Nonfatal Chemical Casualties	Chemical Fatalities	Percentage Fatal
Germany	191,000	9,000	4.5
France	182,000	8,000	4.2
British Empire	180,597	8,109	4.3
United States	71,345	1,462	2.0
Russia	419,340	56,000	11.8

After World War I, governments worldwide thought it desirable to prohibit the use of chemical and biological weapons because of the misery and panic they caused. In 1925, thirty-eight of the countries that belonged to the League of Nations signed the Geneva Protocol for the prohibition of the use in war of asphyxiating, poisonous or other gases, and of bacteriological methods of warfare. Eventually representatives of 130 nations signed the protocol, but there was no way to enforce the agreement because it did not:

• guarantee the abandonment of such weapons because it did not prohibit the manufacture and threat of use of chemical and biological weapons; or

 • **provide for inspections or punishment of signing member countries that violated the agreement.**

Despite the Geneva Protocol, by the time World War II was fought (1939–1945) between the Axis powers—Germany, Italy, and Japan—and the Allies, including France, Great Britain, the Soviet Union, and the United States, most developed countries had stockpiles of chemical and biological weapons and were working on developing new ones. German scientists were responsible for developing many of the lethal nerve agents, including sarin, soman, and tabun, that would later be used by other nations and terrorist groups. When World War II began, Germany had many tons of these agents on hand and was manufacturing even more in numerous chemical weapons plants.

While Germany had a variety of deadly nerve gases they could have used against Allied forces in World War II, they did not use them. The Germans had no way of knowing whether or not the Allies had access to nerve agents, but assumed that they did, and assumed that the Allies would respond in kind if troops were gassed. In fact, British Prime Minister Winston Churchill warned Hitler that if he gassed Allied troops, Great Britain would respond by gassing German troops. This created an unusual stalemate, because both sides believed the other had the largest arsenal of chemical weapons. (But the Allied countries did not know that Germany's stockpile of chemical weapons far exceeded any of their own.)

Even though Great Britain had signed the Geneva Protocol, Churchill came close to using chemical weapons on Germany as World War II progressed. His attitude toward chemical weapons was clear in this 1919 statement made when he was Secretary of State for Great Britain and had authorized the use of chemical weapons against an Iraqi rebellion: "I do not understand this squeamishness about the use of gas. I am strongly in favor of using [it] against uncivilized tribes."

71

While biological agents were used during World War II, especially in prisoner of war camps, their use is not as extensively documented as the use of chemical weapons. Between 1937 and 1945, for instance, it was known that the Japanese in occupied Manchuria, China, infected human prisoners of war with glanders, aerosolized anthrax, yellow fever, plague, cholera, hemorrhagic fevers, and other diseases. This occurred in Unit 731, a facility constructed in China specifically to study the effects of biological weapons on people. Some 10,000 prisoners of war were said to have died as the result of serving as unwilling research subjects.

The Japanese also dropped bombs containing plague-carrying fleas on several areas in China, where several people contracted the disease. (Since plague occurs naturally in China, it was never proved that the Japanese plague attacks were responsible for the outbreak.) While Japan carried out a number of biological weapons attacks, most were probably not successful. At least one attack, involving the release of cholera organisms in a water supply, infected the Japanese troops instead of the enemy, and caused an estimated 10,000 cases of cholera and 1,700 deaths.

At the end of World War II, the victorious Allies seized Germany's stockpile of chemical weapons, including some 20,000 to 30,000 tons (18,144–27,216 metric tons) of tabun. They also took over several chemical plants, one of which was turning out 12,000 tons (10,886 metric tons) of tabun per year. (The use of gas to kill prisoners in concentration camps was well documented after the war, and probably accounts for the quantities manufactured.) Russia seized most of the German chemical weapons manufacturing plants and moved them to Volgograd. This move caused other nations to step up their research on chemical weapons after the war, for fear that Russia would now have a tremendous advantage.

Germany and Japan were not alone in their development of chemical weapons. The United States, even after signing the Geneva Protocol, had steadily increased research and manufacturing of chemical weapons. In December 1941, after the United States declared war on Japan, and Germany declared war on the United States, the United States Chemical Warfare Service received almost unlimited funding. New chemical production facilities were built in the United States, including one at Pine Bluff, Arkansas, and another in Colorado. During World War II, a facility in Dugway, Utah, tested several deadly chemical and biological weapons on mock-ups of Japanese and German buildings.

In 1943, the United States began extensive research into biological weapons, in response to the belief that Germany was prepared to use such weapons against the Allies. The American research was largely conducted at Fort Detrick, Maryland, and at Pine Bluff Arsenal, Arkansas, where pathogens such as anthrax, botulism, various hemorrhagic fever viruses, and other disease organisms and toxins were turned into weapons. These biological weapons could have been used against the Axis powers during World War II, but were not. Fortunately, Russia also chose not to use its huge arsenal of chemical and biological weapons during World War II.

President Franklin D. Roosevelt was reportedly reluctant to consider using poisonous gas against America's enemies during World War II. But because the Japanese had used chemical and biological weapons in Manchuria, China, Roosevelt believed the United States should be prepared to retaliate in kind if the Japanese used such weapons on American troops.

After World War II, research and development of chemical and biological weapons continued in many developed countries. In 1952, for instance, Dr. Ranajit Ghosh, a British scientist, was researching how to develop insecticide chemicals for warfare when he discovered a new poison gas, which he dubbed "VX." VX was more long-lasting and deadly than anything previously discovered. Great Britain gave the formula for VX to the United States, where it was manufactured on a large scale between 1961 and 1968.

In 1969, President Richard M. Nixon issued an executive order that shut down the United States' chemical and biological weapons research facilities. Later, the United States discovered that the U.S.S.R. (now the Russian Federation) had refined its chemical and biological weapons programs and had stockpiled tons of lethal chemicals as well as biological organisms.

In 1972, a ban on the use of biological and chemical weapons was seriously discussed for the first time since the ineffective Geneva Protocol was created after World War I. The Biological and Toxin Weapons Convention (BTWC) held in Geneva resulted in an agreement that prohibited the development or acquisition of biological weapons and any devices to deliver them. Obtaining pathogens for research, however, was not prohibited, and this loophole allowed many nations to obtain lethal organisms under the pretext of research or vaccine programs. Nations were prohibited from stockpiling biological agents, and instructed to destroy existing stockpiles within a certain time period. One hundred forty-three nations eventually signed and ratified the BTWC, but since no provisions were made for conducting inspections to see that signing nations complied with the agreement, it was difficult if not impossible to enforce.

Also in 1972, discussions began at the Geneva-based Chemical Weapons Convention (CWC) to reach an agreement for a permanent ban on chemical weapons. Discussions continued into the 1980s. The CWC banned the production, acquisition, and stockpiling of chemical weapons and also provided for vigorous inspections. Agreement hinged on the inspection process. At first, both the United States and the then U.S.S.R. objected to any intrusive inspections. Finally, by 1987, the two nations agreed to mutual "challenge inspections." This meant that inspectors from both nations could make unannounced inspections of any site without hindrance. Nations began signing the agreement in 1993, and it was finally put into force in 1997.

Not only were chemical and biological weapons used in the two world wars, but their use has also been confirmed or suspected in the following, more recent, conflicts and political incidents:

- **The United States' use of Agent Orange in Vietnam during the 1960s and 1970s is now widely known. Neither the Viet Cong nor North Vietnamese troops used chemicals against the American forces during the Vietnam War.**

- **The Hmong in Laos were reportedly attacked with chemical weapons in the mid-to-late 1970s, though this is unconfirmed.**

- **In 1978, agents of the Bulgarian Communist government killed Georgi Markov, a Bulgarian exile, in London. The device used to kill Markov was the tip of an umbrella that injected a small pellet of ricin toxin (made from castor beans) into his leg while he was waiting for a bus. Markov died several days later.**

- **Soviet troops fighting Afghan rebels in Afghanistan in the 1980s were alleged to have used chemical agents.**

One agent known as Blue-X was said to have immobilized victims for a number of hours. This is unconfirmed.

• The United Nations confirmed in 1984 that Iraq had used mustard gas and tabun more than once against Iran in the war between the two countries from 1980 to 1988. Furthermore, in 1988, Iraq's dictator, Saddam Hussein, also ordered the use of sarin, mustard gas, and cyanide on Kurds living in northern Iraq who were suspected of siding with Iran. This attack killed 4,000 civilians. After this incident was publicized and photographs of the victims circulated, Iran's government agreed to a truce, fearing that Iranians would be so fearful of a chemical attack that they would no longer support the war.

• In 1998, after United States embassies in Nairobi and Tanzania were bombed, the United States retaliated by bombing a pharmaceutical factory in Khartoum allegedly used for producing chemical and biological weapons.

• In 1999, according to a report by the Inter Press Service, the United Nations sent a team of physicians to Nairobi to treat hundreds of civilians who were suffering from symptoms thought to be caused by chemical weapons. A rebel group in south Sudan, the Sudan People's Liberation Army, accused the Sudanese government of dispersing the toxic chemicals during bombing missions over the towns of Lanya and Kaya. After the bombing runs, citizens of the two towns suffered sore eyes, sore throats, and disorientation. Some vomited blood. Large numbers of cattle, sheep, goats, and birds in the area also died.

• An unknown person(s) carried out the 2001 anthrax attacks in the United States.

• American veterans of the 1990–1991 Persian Gulf War between the United States and Iraq have reported a variety of symptoms, including nausea, cramps, rashes, fatigue, headaches, joint and muscle pain, short-term memory loss, difficulty breathing, and birth defects in their newborns. The symptoms, when not attributed to another illness or condition, are called the Gulf War syndrome. While the United States has denied that Iraq used chemical or biological agents, other sources attribute Gulf War Syndrome to exposure to these weapons. (After the war, five biological warfare facilities with stockpiles of anthrax, botulism, and gas gangrene bacteria were found in Iraq.) In 1996, the United States government said that Gulf War soldiers may have been exposed to chemical and biological agents when production facilities in Iraq were bombed.

While we can hope that chemical and biological weapons will not be used again, most military experts agree that world events have increased the possibility of a chemical or biological attack. These events include the following:

1. Since the Cold War ended, unstable economic conditions in the former Soviet Union have meant that many scientists and military personnel are not paid enough to support themselves or their families. These conditions have forced specialists in the production of chemical and biological weapons to seek employment elsewhere—often in countries wanting to use such weapons.

2. The rise of fanatical religious groups worldwide with the mindset that there are infidels (people who disagree with certain religious beliefs or who have no religious beliefs) in the world who must be purged has contributed to the threat of the use of chemical and biological weapons.

3. State-sponsored terrorism in several countries allows those nations to damage others in terrorist attacks, without fighting an all-out war. The blurring of distinctions between terrorism and conventional warfare makes terrorism, to some nations, an acceptable alternative.

4. The changing concept of war, from conflicts that last for years to those that are over in days, makes terrorism seem a feasible way to fight a war.

5. The increasing prices of conventional weapons make chemical and biological warfare seem a more economical alternative.

In many cases, an attacker's circumstances may dictate the use of chemical and biological weapons. For example, if one does not have an air force to attack a United States military base, the base might still be knocked out by contaminating its food or water supplies to produce widespread dysentery (a severe, disabling diarrhea).

6

Tests and Accidents

In 1992, after serving seventeen years as head of Russia's Biopreparat, the agency charged with developing and producing biological weapons, Ken Alibek (formerly Kanatjan Alibekov) defected with his family to the United States. There he revealed to the U.S. government the extent of the Russian Federation's biological and chemical weapons programs. Although American authorities knew that the Russians had continued developing and storing chemical and biological weapons even after agreeing to scuttle those programs and destroy their stockpiles, the programs Alibek described went far beyond anything imagined. The Soviets had stored tons of chemical and biological weapons and maintained active programs where chemical and biological agents were perfected, tested, and produced. In his book, *Biohazard*, Alibek describes an island in the Aral Sea where Russia tested biological weapons on monkeys:

> One hundred monkeys are tethered to posts set in parallel rows stretching out toward the horizon. A muffled thud breaks the stillness. Far in the distance, a small metal sphere lifts into the sky then hurtles downward, rotating, until it shatters in a second explosion.
>
> Some seventy-five feet above the ground, a cloud the color of dark mustard begins to unfurl, gently dissolving as it glides down toward the monkeys. They pull at their chains and begin to cry. Some bury their heads between their legs. A few cover their mouths or noses, but it is too late: they have already begun to die.

Alibek then describes how a small group of observers wearing biological protective suits watch from a distance. They retrieve those monkeys who are still breathing and take them to laboratories where they are observed until they die of anthrax, tularemia, Q fever, brucellosis, glanders, or plague—just a few of the many biological and chemical agents tested on the island.

These tests seem cruel, but many countries have used animal or human subjects to test chemical and biological weapons. In addition, primates and other animals are often used to test the vaccines developed as protection against biological agents. Whatever one's feelings about animal testing, this is probably a necessary step if we are to be assured that vaccines are safe before they are administered to humans.

When military personnel or civilians have been used as test subjects some have consented, but at other times subjects have been unsuspecting. And despite scientists' and military personnel precautions, as chemical and biological weapons are developed, handled, stored, and released they have at times caused tragic accidents.

During World War I, for example, the Russians decided to use chemical weapons against German soldiers for the first time in July 1916. Gas canisters were to be opened at midnight, but for some unknown reason, the first release took place at 3:00 A.M. The Germans detected the gas and issued warnings to their troops. The wind was beginning to change direction, meaning that the gas would be blown back toward Russian troops in their trenches, but a second wave of gas was ordered to be released anyway. The wind continued to change, and when a third wave of gas was released it blew straight into Russian trenches. Three hundred Russian soldiers were killed by their own gas attacks. At the end of World War I, the Russians had suffered 419,340 injured and 56,000 dead from chemical weapons alone. (The Russians suffered more deaths from gas because they were slow to develop an effective gas mask.)

Nations have also learned through unfortunate experiences that it is dangerous to keep large stockpiles of chemical weapons. Storage containers can leak, mixtures are often volatile and can be ignited by careless workers or other sources, and so on. One such accident happened during World War II. On December 2, 1943, an American ship, the SS *John Harvey*, was docked at the Bari harbor in southern Italy waiting to unload. In addition to its regular cargo, the ship was secretly carrying 2,000 mustard gas bombs. While the SS *John Harvey* waited at the dock, the German Luftwaffe attacked the harbor. The planes bombed and sank seventeen ships and damaged eight more. A thousand soldiers were killed and another 800 were injured. The SS *John Harvey* was sinking when the gas containers onboard ruptured, spreading mustard gas over the water. Six hundred thirty of the skip's crew were blinded and burned.

Seventy of them died. Civilian casualties were also high, due to clouds of vaporized mustard gas that moved ashore as the *SS John Harvey* sank.

In the United States, many chemical and biological weapons were tested at the Dugway Proving Grounds, located about 80 miles from Salt Lake City, Utah. In 1969, a plane spraying the nerve agent VX over mock-ups of buildings on the ground failed to close the vent that was spraying the gas during a turn, accidentally releasing about 20 pounds (9 kg) of the chemical. The mistake caused the gas to blow over an area where sheep grazed, and some 6,300 sheep were killed. No humans were killed or injured, but the incident was costly and embarrassing for the United States government.

More recently, in November 1979, the world learned that there had been a serious outbreak of anthrax in the Siberian town of Sverdlovsk around April first of that year. While the Carter administration in the United States was certain there had been an accident at a bioweapons plant, which was proof that the Russian government was violating the 1972 BTWC, the Russians denied the allegations. They said the outbreak of anthrax was caused by contaminated meat.

It was eventually made public that workers at the Sverdlovsk bioweapons plant had forgotten to replace a clogged filter on an exhaust pipe in the anthrax-drying department. The pipe pumped air out of the plant, and a filter was necessary to catch any anthrax spores that were in the air inside the plant. The filter was removed during one shift, and a note was left to remind the next shift to replace the filter. When workers forgot to replace the pipe's filter, for several hours countless numbers of anthrax spores were pumped out of the plant and carried across the town by the wind. The missing filter was finally replaced, but plant workers did not report the incident. Three to four days after the accident, hospitals began admitting dozens of people who had lived and worked in the vicinity of the plant. According to Soviet officials, ninety-six people fell ill with anthrax, and sixty-six of them died.

The incident was never fully explained to the people of Sverdlovsk or to the outside world. In his 1990 autobiography *Against the Grain*, Boris Yeltsin, former president of Russia (1990–1999), referred to the Sverdlovsk anthrax epidemic in one of the book's footnotes as the result of a "leak from a secret factory."

While civilians and military personnel have been exposed to chemical and biological weapons by accident, they have also been intentionally exposed as part of weapons tests. For instance, between 1963 and 1970, members of the U.S. Marine Corps, Navy, Army and Air Force took part in a series of tests code-named Project SHAD (Shipboard Hazard and Defense). The tests involved spraying about 4,300 American soldiers aboard barges, tugs, destroyers, and other ships with sarin, VX, and biological toxins that caused flu-like symptoms. Project SHAD tests were intended to reveal how well U.S. warships could defend against chemical and biological agents and still remain war-ready. The soldiers onboard the ships wore protective gear, but did not realize they were being exposed to actual nerve and biological agents. Many later reported health problems. In July 2002, U.S. Pentagon and Veterans Affairs officials released information concerning the 1960s tests and announced that veterans who have health problems linked to Project SHAD could apply for disability compensation.

In October 2002, the U.S. government revealed that twenty-eight chemical and biological weapons had been tested on U.S. soil during the 1960s, at locations including Alaska, Maryland, Florida, and Hawaii. The tests were directed from the Deseret Test Center, headquartered at Fort Douglas, Utah. In one test, sarin and VX were released from used artillery shells and bombs. Other tests described by the Pentagon in 2002 included:

- **Devil Hole I, a test designed to show how well sarin gas would disperse in aspen and spruce forests after** being released from artillery shells and rockets. The tests were conducted during the summer of **1965** at the Gerstle River test site in Alaska.

• **Devil Hole II**, also conducted at the Gerstle River site in Alaska, which tested how well the nerve agent VX was dispersed from artillery shells. Mannequins dressed in military uniforms and placed in military trucks were used in the tests.

• **Big Tom**, a 1965 test that involved spraying bacteria over the Hawaiian Island of Oahu. The purpose of the test was to develop responses to a biological attack. The bacterium used, *Bacillus globigii*, was considered harmless at the time, but was later found to cause infections in people with weakened immune systems.

Testing has often been done in secret, with the test subjects unaware that they have been exposed to chemical or biological weapons. For instance, a mold named *Coccidioides immitis* is known to form spores suitable for use in aerosols. It is also considered more likely to cause illness in certain ethnic groups. In the 1950s, the United States reportedly performed controversial tests of the mold on African-American subjects.

A history of secret human experimentation, including tests involving chemical and biological weapons, was posted on the Health News Network Web site in October 2002. The list included tests conducted from 1931 through 1997 and other events related to human experimentation.

Here are a few of the CBW tests from the list of those that were performed in the United States:

1942: The Chemical Warfare Services conducts mustard gas tests on about 4,000 soldiers. Religion-based conscientious objectors were reportedly used in the tests.

1944: The Navy uses human subjects placed in locked chambers to test gas masks and protective clothing against mustard gas exposure.

1947: The Central Intelligence Agency (CIA) uses civilians and military personnel as unknowing test subjects to study the use of LSD, a mind-altering drug, as a potential weapon.

1950: The Navy sprays an American city with a biological agent to determine susceptibility to a biological attack. Monitoring devices are placed throughout the city to track the spread of the organism. Many residents report pneumonia-like symptoms.

1953: The following areas are exposed to zinc cadmium sulfide gas in military tests to determine how efficiently chemical agents could be dispersed: Winnipeg, Manitoba, Canada; St. Louis, Missouri; Minneapolis, Minnesota; Fort Wayne, Indiana; Leesburg, Virginia; and certain areas in Maryland.

1955: The CIA tests its ability to infect human populations with biological agents by releasing a type of bacteria from the Army's biological warfare stock over Tampa Bay, Florida.

1965: Prisoners at the Holmesburg State Prison in Philadelphia are exposed to dioxin, the toxic chemical found in Agent Orange.

1966: The Army releases *Bacillus subtilis* variant *niger* in the New York City subway system, exposing more than a million people to the organism.

IN JUNE 1998, AT THE NEVADA TEST SITE IN MERCURY, NEVADA, A TRAINING EXERCISE AT THE HAZARDOUS MATERIAL SPILL CENTER SIMULATED A TERRORIST ATTACK WHERE AN EXPLOSIVE DEVICE UNLEASHED THE TOXIC CHEMICAL **VX.**

In addition to those tests, examination of clinical cases of soldiers and civilians who had been exposed to chemical and biological weapons during warfare has provided information about the effects of such weapons. Animal research has also contributed to the fund of knowledge about chemical and biological weapons, including vaccines, treatments, and antidotes for exposure.

The U.S. government maintains that the testing of chemical and biological weapons has continued to the present simply as a protective measure—to determine antidotes, treatments, and vaccines for these agents.

In the late 1980s, as Iraq was preparing to invade Kuwait, it tested and produced artillery shells, bombs, and missile warheads that could be loaded with biological warheads. In 1988, tests produced a cloud of botulinum that killed animals on a test range. Around the same time, Iraq's scientists successfully tested an aerosol generator mounted on a military helicopter, dispensing bacteria similar to anthrax.

In 1989, the Iraqis tested a biological bomb that was delivered by airplane and floated down to its target by parachute. Some of the bombs were filled with anthrax and some with botulinum. The bombs and missiles were crude and when exploded usually killed most of the pathogens. The Iraqis also tested a container that could be filled with anthrax or botulinum and sprayed from a plane. If it were used on humans, American scientists declared that this weapon would have been more effective than the bombs and missiles loaded with toxic agents that Iraq had tested. After the Gulf War ceasefire, Saddam Hussein said all of these weapons and more had been destroyed, but no documentation was provided to prove that this had been done.

7

Protecting Soldiers from Chemical and Biological Weapons

Important objectives of testing biological and chemical weapons include devising body suits and face masks to protect soldiers from the effects of exposure to pathogens and toxic chemicals, and creating drugs and vaccines to counter the effects of CBWs or to prevent disease.

Just as the first uses of chemical and biological weapons date back several centuries, so do the first attempts at protection against chemical and biological agents. Leonardo da Vinci once designed a mask that was simply cloth dipped in water. To protect themselves from the plague, scientists in the 1600s used cone-shaped masks that resembled birds' beaks. The cones were filled with various spices and herbs.

In 1849, inventor Lewis P. Haslett received a U.S. patent for his Lung-Protector, a wool mask dipped in water. Shortly thereafter, various masks were devised that were made out of rubber and used charcoal as a filtering agent. In 1912, an American named Garrett A. Morgan invented a gas mask for firemen and engineers called the Morgan Safety Hood and Smoke Protector. However, it did not protect against gases used in warfare.

The German inventor, Alexander B. Drager, patented one of the first gas masks for soldiers in 1914. Drager's mask used layers of pads soaked in bicarbonate and sodium thiosulfate, with charcoal between the pad layers. The German mask was superior to the device used by the British at the beginning of World War I. They wore water-soaked gauze pads over their noses and mouths, held in place by the same type of veiling used on ladies' hats. By 1916, however, the British had developed PH helmets, consisting of flannel hoods that had eyepieces soaked in glycerin and sodium thiosulfate.

The PH helmet differed from earlier versions in that it had an expiratory valve, and the cloth was treated with chemicals that could destroy phosgene gas. (The active ingredient was hexamethylenetetramine.) The French M2 mask was similar to the British mask, consisting of layers of chemically treated cloth that the air passed through as the wearer breathed.

By early 1916, German soldiers had a more functional gas mask. These masks, called *gummischutzmasken* in German, had metal filtering canisters that were either attached directly to the face piece (made of canvas, rubber, or leather) or connected to it by a corrugated rubber tube.

Some of the early masks with such filtering systems required the wearer to use nose clips and breathe through a snorkel-like device held between the jaws. The Americans adopted this type of mask in 1916 after the United States entered the First World War.

Most early masks were uncomfortable, heavy, and unbearably hot. A tight fit was essential, and the masks often had glass eyepieces that fogged over as the wearer breathed and carbon dioxide built up inside the mask. American soldiers were told never to remove their gas masks until an officer gave the command to do so, but when breathing became difficult and they could no longer see through the eyepieces, they often tore off their masks, sometimes with tragic results.

During World War I, horses transported men and supplies, and they wore specially tailored gas masks. Soldiers were told to put horses' gas masks on first during a gas attack, because a horse couldn't be taught to hold its breath.

Dogs used during World War I also wore gas masks made especially for them.

Masks and respirators were redesigned many times between 1900 and 1950.

When World War II broke out in 1939, there was a general expectation that chemical weapons would be used again, as they had been during World War I. This time, however, the troops were prepared. Both the Allied and the Axis powers had been stockpiling chemical and biological weapons, and they had also been improving protective gear for soldiers to use against such agents. Soldiers now had masks with fully molded face pieces, diaphragms allowing speech, optical sighting devices, microphone attachments and inner nose cups to reduce fogging. American, Japanese, and British troops wore masks as part of their training. They fully expected to use them as the war progressed.

Schoolchildren in London were issued gas masks, and in Germany, mothers and children could requisition special capes and masks for protection against possible gas attacks. In the United States, Walt Disney helped design a Mickey Mouse gas mask so that if the war was brought to U.S. soil and children had to wear gas masks, they wouldn't be afraid of them.

A *DESIGNED FOR LIVING* POSTER BY SASCHA MAURER REMINDS WORLD WAR II SOLDIERS TO TAKE GOOD CARE OF THEIR LIFE-SAVING GAS MASKS.

Full-scale chemical warfare, however, was never initiated during World War II. The war ended on August 6, 1945, when the United States dropped atomic bombs on Hiroshima and Nagasaki, Japan, thus ushering in the nuclear age. For the next decade people around the world so feared a nuclear attack that they built and stocked bomb shelters and conducted "duck and cover" drills for schoolchildren. During these drills, schoolchildren crouched under their desks, arms hugging their heads, until the all-clear signal was given.

In 1945, Korea was divided into North and South sections at the thirty-eighth parallel. Communist North Korea formed a militant regime, armed by the Union of Soviet Socialist Republics (U.S.S.R.). In June 1950, North Korea invaded South Korea. The United Nations declared North Korea the aggressor and sent troops (made up mostly of American soldiers) to defend South Korea. China sent troops to fight with the North Koreans, and in 1953, when it was clear neither side could win, an armistice was signed and the war ended. During the Korean War, also called the Korean Conflict, all American soldiers were issued gas masks and routinely trained for the possibility of facing chemical and biological weapons. Chemical and biological weapons were not used on a large scale in the Korean War, but there is evidence that the United States may have used experimental biological weapons.

The Cold War between the United States and the Soviet Union was in full swing during the 1950s and 1960s, and both nations continued to develop and stockpile chemical and biological weapons. Smaller nations also accumulated stockpiles of such weapons. Because of this, protective gear was constantly under improvement, and vaccines against some biological weapons and antidotes to some nerve gases were developed. Respiratory masks now had more effective filters and fit the faces of those who wore them better than before. The improved gas masks were used, to a limited extent, during the Vietnam War.

The Korean War ended in 1953, and a year later war broke out between Communist North Vietnam and noncommunist South Vietnam, two parts of what was once French Indochina. U.S. President Dwight D. Eisenhower and his successors, John F. Kennedy and Lyndon B. Johnson, sent increasing numbers of American military advisors and troops to Vietnam. Although war was never officially declared, American soldiers fought there until President Richard M. Nixon withdrew U.S. troops in 1973.

During the Vietnam War, American troops used tear gas to flush enemy soldiers from underground tunnels. American soldiers who searched enemy tunnels filled with tear gas wore the M28 protective mask, a lightweight mask worn when nerve agents were not a problem. Gas masks were not routinely issued to American troops, since Viet Cong and North Vietnamese troops did not use chemical weapons. However, the Americans sprayed Agent Orange over the countryside to kill crops supplying enemy troops with food and to reduce the thick vegetation where the enemy could hide. Since the United States did not consider tear gas and Agent Orange chemical *weapons*, they did not consider their use banned by international agreements. (The United States considered these substances helpful chemicals, but did not believe they could kill or disable enemy troops, so did not classify them as weapons.)

By the time the war was over, about 60,000 American soldiers had been killed in Vietnam and another 304,704 wounded.

Throughout the 1990s, the United States continued to do research on improved protective gear for soldiers facing potential chemical and biological weapons. New gas masks could filter smoke, in addition to other agents. Masks were also eventually developed that could filter biological agents from inhaled air. Protective clothing improved until it was nearly as functional as the suits used by astronauts in outer space, and could protect wearers from both chemical and biological agents and even radiation from nuclear weapons.

By the time U.S. and North Atlantic Treaty Organization (NATO) troops were sent to fight in the Persian Gulf (1990–1991) after Iraq's dictator Saddam Hussein ordered his army to attack neighboring Kuwait, they were well prepared for chemical and biological attacks. American troops were vaccinated against anthrax, smallpox, and other diseases before they were sent to the Middle East. They were also issued M17A2 gas masks and full body protective suits. Chemical detection and decontamination equipment was carried by many of the American troops. In addition, because of Israel's proximity to Iraq and Hussein's expressed hatred toward the Jewish state, thousands of gas masks were issued to Israeli citizens, in case Iraq launched chemical or biological weapons against Israel.

Most experts agree that new technologies have made the prospect of chemical and biological warfare, and by extension, terrorism, more frightening, because the agents available for use are now more lethal. But new technologies have also given us the ability to more adequately protect our military and our civilian population from such attacks.

Modern gas mask technology, for instance, has given rise to new protective gear that far surpasses anything available through the 1990s. After the Gulf War, when respirators were still too awkward and uncomfortable to wear in the desert heat, researchers worked on developing protective gear that did not hinder a soldier's movement or ability to fight. The result were ultra lightweight masks and form-fitting body suits that could be worn for extensive time periods without causing discomfort or hindering movement. Mesh, form-fitting headpieces have replaced rubber and elastic head straps for holding masks over the face. The new design leaves the ears uncovered, but protects the face and most of the head. Two exchangeable filters can be switched one at a time while soldiers are in the field, providing constant protection without removing the mask. New respirators also provide for voice communication and include drinking devices and optical inserts for the soldier's convenience and comfort.

Mask-testing equipment is also available. The small device connects to the mask, allowing the mask wearer to test for a tight fit. The fit-tester measures dust in the outside air, as compared to dust that has entered the mask, if any.

Unfortunately, until all nations observe treaties calling for the destruction of chemical and biological weapon stockpiles, protective gear will remain a vital part of the soldier's wartime paraphernalia.

"As the new millennium approaches,
we face the very real and increasing prospect
that regional aggressors, third-rate armies,
terrorist groups and even religious cults
will seek to wield disproportionate power
by acquiring and using [weapons of mass destruction]."

Former U.S. Secretary of Defense William Cohen, 1997

8

Control and Disarmament

Most national governments want the research into and the production of chemical and biological weapons stopped and all stockpiles destroyed; therefore, efforts have been made over the years to control the production and use of chemical and biological weapons. The problem remains, however, that as long as there are benefits to be gained by using chemical and biological weapons, and as long as any nation suspects other nations of secretly producing and stockpiling them, the race to develop them will probably continue.

Several international conferences over the last century have attempted to set boundaries concerning warfare. For instance, approximately a hundred years ago, the First Hague Conference (1899) and the Second Hague Conference (1907) held in The Netherlands were called by Russia for the purpose of setting certain rules of war. Neither conference succeeded in the announced purpose of convincing nations to reduce armaments, but other provisions were ratified. For instance, prohibitions were passed concerning the use of submarine mines, aerial bombardment, and poison gas. The conferences also addressed the issues of recognizing the neutrality of ships on the high seas and protecting civilians during a war. However, since there were no provisions made for inspections or penalties, these prohibitions proved ineffective and were largely ignored during and after World War I.

After the extensive use of chemical weapons in World War I, the Geneva Protocol, as discussed in Chapter 5, attempted to limit the use of toxic gases and biological weapons in warfare. But, again, due to the absence of provisions for inspections and penalties, the agreement proved ineffective in reducing production, stockpiling, and the use of chemical and biological weapons.

Four conventions held in Geneva in 1949 again set rules for conducting war. The first two conventions mandated humane treatment for the wounded, sick, and shipwrecked during wartime. The third and fourth conventions set forth rules for dealing humanely with prisoners of war. Other treaties and conventions between 1925 and 1972 dealt with such issues as the protection of cultural property during war, the Antarctic, banning nuclear weapons tests, and governing activities of states in exploring and using outer space. These conferences did not address chemical and biological weapons.

In 1969 and 1970, President Richard M. Nixon issued a National Security Directive ordering a halt to all offensive development and production of biological weapons. Consequently, by 1972, the United States had destroyed most of its biological weapons stocks and delivery systems. All American research in biological weapons was also discontinued, and research facilities were closed, destroyed, or converted to other uses. Nixon's directives set the stage for the 1972 Geneva Convention on the Prohibition of the Development, Production and Stockpiling of Bacteriological (Biological) and Toxin Weapons and on their Destruction (BTWC).

The prohibition of biological weapons was addressed in April 1972 at the BTWC. The convention reinforced the provisions of the Geneva Protocol and called upon all ratifying nations "for the sake of all mankind" to eliminate from their arsenals "such dangerous weapons of mass destruction as those using chemical or bacteriological (biological) agents. . . ."

The preamble to the convention made it clear why such a resolution was necessary: "[We are] convinced that such use [of chemical and biological weapons] would be repugnant to the conscience of mankind and that no effort should be spared to minimize this risk. . . ."

Convention participants agreed not to "develop, produce, stockpile or otherwise acquire or retain":

- **microbial or other biological agents, or toxins whatever their origin or method of production, of types and in quantities that have no justification for prophylactic, protective or other peaceful purposes; or**

- **weapons, equipment, or means of delivery designed to use such agents or toxins for hostile purposes or in armed conflict.**

The Convention participants also agreed to destroy, "or to divert to peaceful purposes," all biological weapons and equipment for delivery of those weapons not later than nine months after the agreement took effect. One hundred forty nations signed and ratified the agreement, and it went into effect March 26, 1975. The United States and other Western nations complied, until they realized that at least ten other nations had not done so, but instead had accelerated their biological weapons programs. Again, no provisions were made for inspections or penalties to help ensure compliance. Furthermore, the provision that biological agents could be kept for "peaceful purposes," such as making vaccines, was a loophole that some nations used to continue their biological weapons programs.

The United States had tried to comply with most of the provisions of the BTWC, but had maintained the part of its biological weapons program that was vital to defense.

The U.S. government had long suspected that Russia was continuing its chemical and biological weapons programs, not just for defense, but to produce more lethal chemical and biological weapons. This was confirmed when Ken Alibek, a scientist with Russia's biological weapons program, defected to the United States in 1992. Alibek emphasized to U.S. government officials just how much Russia's biological weapons program had grown even after that country had signed the 1972 BTWC agreement.

In *Germs*, the authors recount the information Alibek relayed to the government during two months of debriefings: "Moscow," he reported in grim detail, "had secretly produced hundreds of tons of anthrax, smallpox, and plague germs meant for use against the United States and its allies. The amounts dwarfed anything American experts had ever imagined." (Another source said Russia maintained a 4,500-metric ton supply of weapon-quality anthrax at all times.) Other sources emphasize that listing metric tons of biological organisms produced by a nation is not useful information, because biological agents are more accurately measured by concentration. For example, an anthrax culture might contain 5,000 spores per milliliter, which would be a more lethal concentration in a small amount of material than if it consisted of 500 spores per ton.

Alibek also outlined Russia's huge "germ empire," which included the Soviet Council of Ministers, the Soviet Academy of Sciences, the Ministries of Defense, Health, and Agriculture, and the Biopreparat, the so-called civilian pharmaceutical agency that employed Alibek and tens of thousands of other scientists and workers at more than forty sites in Russia and Kazakhstan.

After William J. (Bill) Clinton's inauguration as president in January 1993, he quickly learned that the United States faced a new and serious threat when Islamic terrorists bombed the World Trade Center in New York City. The blast killed six and injured almost a thousand. The 1993 attack did not collapse the towers, as the terrorists perhaps hoped it would, but it severely damaged the building and its underground parking garage. Clinton often stated how much worse the 1993 attack on the World Trade Center would have been if the explosive device had also contained a deadly biological agent or poison gas.

Shortly after his inauguration, President Clinton learned that the threat posed by chemical and biological weapons was also magnified by the fact that many scientists who were unemployed after the collapse of the Soviet Union might be tempted, for large salaries, to help other nations or terrorist groups develop weapons of mass destruction.

Clinton, therefore, pushed for American-Russian cooperation in biological research for peaceful purposes. Russian scientists toured biological research facilities in the United States, and in 1998 American scientists and state department officials were invited to visit Vector, Russia's Siberian virus facility. Americans eventually visited Building 6 in the huge, one-hundred-building complex, a top-secret facility that housed smallpox laboratories, aerosol test chambers, and a restricted laboratory where research on other agents was underway.

Promised American funding for future research collaboration, the Russians agreed to stop producing biological weapons and to work with American scientists on peace-oriented projects. However, since Russia's four military labs still remained closed to Western officials, there was no way to know what kind of research was carried on there. In the late 1990s, U.S. government officials worried that Russia not only was continuing research on biological weapons, but also now had access to American funding and expertise.

Since genetic engineering was progressing with amazing speed, the Clinton administration knew that it could be possible to manipulate the DNA of deadly disease organisms to create a super biological weapon—a formidable weapon against which victims would have no defense. In fact, Russians scientists claimed to have accomplished such a feat by combining smallpox organisms with Marburg fever, one of the extremely deadly hemorrhagic fever organisms. If such reports were true, this new organism could cause a highly contagious, horrific disease for which there would be no effective vaccine or treatment.

With all of this on his mind, Clinton allocated more government funds for prevention and preparedness, and his administration continued to work with Russia to prevent that country from expanding its chemical and biological weapons research and facilities. The U.S. government also structured its chemical and biological weapons program to conform to BTWC rules.

In the meantime, the World Health Organization (WHO) recommended in 1996 that all remaining smallpox cultures in the world be destroyed by 2000. WHO was referring to cultures that had either been sent to WHO repositories or retained at the CDC in Atlanta or at Vector in Siberia when worldwide vaccination programs were proclaimed to have defeated smallpox. The United States and Russia refused to destroy their cultures, claiming they needed them for research and to produce vaccine in the event of a biological attack. WHO then extended the deadline for destruction to 2002, but since the anthrax attacks in the United States in 2001, the government may again be reluctant to comply.

As discussed in Chapter 5, a ban on chemical weapons was first proposed in 1972 and finally put into effect in 1997. The years of delay were due primarily to failure to agree on "intrusive" inspections. Neither the United States nor the Russian Federation and its allies, the two largest producers of chemical weapons, wanted foreign inspectors looking into their chemical stockpiles. The Cold War ended during this period, however, and the two nations finally agreed to inspections.

Its authors having learned valuable lessons from the Geneva Protocol, the 1972 Chemical Weapons Convention (CWC) was written more forcefully than the previous agreement. It listed in detail those chemicals and their precursors (ingredients used to make deadly chemicals) that were banned. The CWC prohibited the "development, production, acquisition, retention, stockpiling, transfer and use of all chemical weapons." Nations that signed and ratified the CWC were required to declare all chemicals stockpiled. They were also required to destroy all chemical weapons within a certain time period—usually five to ten years, depending on each nation's circumstances. Each nation was responsible for cleaning up chemical weapons left in other countries, and was also required to destroy or convert chemical weapon manufacturing plants in existence since 1946 to peacetime use.

The 1993 CWC provided for an organization of ratifying nations—the Organization for the Prohibition of Chemical Weapons (OPCW)—based in The Hague, to oversee compliance.

The CWC has been continually debated and amended, but is still the most effective worldwide ban on chemical weapons. Stockpiles of toxic chemicals and facilities for making them in the United States (deadline 2004), Russia (deadline 2007), and other nations have been destroyed, and destruction will continue for several years.

When George W. Bush became president in January 2001, the cooperative effort between the United States and Russia was falling apart. Plans to use one of Russia's largest bioweapons facilities to make disposable syringes and sterilize syringes did not occur because of unpaid utility bills and shortages of materials in Russia.

As former bioweapons facilities were destroyed, many Russian scientists lost their jobs. Despite the 1972 BTWC, Iran, Iraq, and other countries actively recruited these scientists to help with chemical and biological weapons programs. The problem remains, and there is evidence that a few Russian scientists, understandably, have given in to the offers of high salaries and luxurious living conditions and are helping some nations improve their chemical and biological weapons programs.

For three decades, the nations concerned about the possibility of facing biological weapons attacks have been working on revisions to the 1972 BTWC that would make the agreement easier to enforce. A recent amendment to the treaty would require nations to list laboratories where advanced research was being done and submit to regular inspections.

The U.S. Department of Commerce feared that the new provisions of the BTWC would give pharmaceutical companies unfair access to competitors' research. In addition, government officials felt that even intrusive inspections would not prevent rogue nations from working on biological weapons because it is easy to make chemical and biological weapons facilities and production equipment appear to be used for consumer purposes, such as vaccines and insecticides, when they are actually being used to produce chemical and biological weapons. (Observe the ease with which Iraq was able to hide chemical and biological weapons work from a United Nations team of inspectors after the Gulf War ended in 1991.)

Therefore, in 2001, the Bush administration refused to approve the changes to the BTWC. The refusal was widely criticized by other countries, including our traditional allies, Great Britain and Japan.

As worldwide agreements to ban chemical and biological weapons were being discussed and revised, the U.S. government was moving to make deadly organism cultures harder to obtain. For instance, as a direct result of the first arrest of Larry Wayne Harris in 1995 for falsifying a mail order request for plague cultures, in 1996 Congress passed a law prohibiting the domestic transfer of pathogens, except to confirmed scientists and medical researchers. The law also made it illegal to threaten a biological attack. (A 1989 law banned exports of certain biological organisms to countries that might use them as weapons, such as Iran and Iraq.)

Since safeguarding legitimately held pathogen cultures is the best way to keep them out of the wrong hands, the 1996 law also made it more difficult for anyone to obtain twenty-four infectious agents and twelve toxins, including anthrax, bubonic plague, tularemia, and brucellosis. Shippers and receivers of any of these agents would need to register with the CDC. This meant that the American laboratories that keep biological organisms would have to register with the CDC and would also have to allow federal inspections.

The CWC's provision for scheduled and "challenge" (meaning on short notice) inspections is perhaps the best way to keep nations from continuing chemical weapons production. Inspectors can look for a variety of signs that a chemical weapons plant exists, without seeing the plant itself. Here are a few:

- **changes in the environment around the site of a chemical weapons plant, including a high number of dead or dying plants, or large numbers of dying fish in a pond or stream;**

- **excessive growth of algae in ponds receiving water runoff from a plant. This would most likely be due to abnormally high phosphorous levels in the chemical runoff;**

- **the presence in soil of high levels of chemicals used to make chemical weapons around the area of a suspected chemical weapons facility;**

- **if the plant itself is inspected, glass and Teflon tanks may indicate chemical weapons production because metal tanks are corroded by the chemicals and could not be used.**

Some of these signs, however, could also be present in a legitimate chemical production facility, making the detection process extremely difficult in many cases.

After World War II, the Allies dumped tons of Germany's chemical weapons stockpiles into the Baltic Sea. Japan disposed of its stockpiles in similar fashion off its coast. Rockets and missiles loaded with chemicals have been detonated in uninhabited areas where the chemicals could fade away over time.

Under the 1986 U.S. Department of Defense Authorization Act, the United States must destroy all of its chemical weapons stockpiles by 2004. Today, destruction of chemical and biological weapons stockpiles inside the

United States must observe environmental law. Chemical-laden warheads are separated from firing mechanisms, then burned at high temperatures. The gases from this incineration process are "scrubbed" with filters and rendered inert. The rockets or bombs used to carry the chemical loads are disarmed and destroyed.

According to Dr. Pilch of the Monterey Institute's Center for Nonproliferation Studies, in the United States, destruction of biological weapons in 1971 after termination of the U.S. Biological Weapons Program was done this way:

1. Biological cultures in liquid form were sterilized in tanks, by heating with steam to 280 degrees Fahrenheit (138 °C) for three hours.

2. The samples were tested to ensure that the agent had been destroyed. In the United States, the CDC verified test results.

3. After verification that the agent had been destroyed, sewage organisms were added and the material was biodegraded.

4. The material was sterilized again.

5. The material was tested again.

6. The material was placed in drums and sterilized in an autoclave, which is an appliance that can be set to high temperatures to kill organisms.

7. The material, now harmless, was transported to a commercial sewage treatment facility for further biodegradation.

8. The material was taken to a sealed evaporation pond and allowed to dry.

9. The material was collected, spread on a designated location, disked into the soil to a depth of four inches, and covered with grass. (In the United States, this material was taken to the former bioweapons facility at Pine Bluff Arsenal, Arkansas, and buried there.)

The BTWC has not been as successful as the CWC in requiring nations to comply with disarmament, since inspections are not required. If inspections were to be required, some sources believe they would be inconclusive in most cases, because equipment used in pharmaceutical, food, beverage, and other industries is also used to produce biological warfare agents. And a conversion from consumer to weapons uses can be made quickly.

Russia no longer cooperates with attempts by the United States and Great Britain to hold mutual inspections of biological research facilities, so it is unclear whether Russia continues research in biological weapons.

While most nations that signed and ratified the BTWC and CWC are adhering to its provisions, a close watch must be kept because there is always the chance that nations will cheat to gain the advantage that chemical and biological weapons might provide during war or a terrorist attack.

In 1984, thirty-three nations formed the Australia Group, which is dedicated to stopping the proliferation of chemical and biological weapons. The nations within the group had learned that Iraq, Iran, and Libya had obtained the supplies and equipment for CBWs programs from the international marketplace. Consequently, the group decided to monitor chemical manufacturing facilities, technology, and sales. The chemical industry cooperated with the Australia Group, and the Government-Industry Conference against Chemical Weapons was the result. The conference meets twice a year in Paris to exchange information and review measures to halt the growth of chemical and biological weapons production.

Iraq's chemical and biological weapons programs have remained a problem since the Gulf War. After the war ended in 1991, the United Nations formed the United Nations Special Commission (UNSCOM). The Commission gave inspection teams the task of inspecting Iraq's chemical and biological warfare plants to ensure that they were either being destroyed or converted to peacetime use, in compliance with the Gulf War cease fire agreement. Inspectors were kept out of several sites, but indications were that Iraq did have production facilities and

UNDER THE SUPERVISION OF UNITED NATIONS INSPECTORS, IRAQI WORKERS DESTROY A NUCLEAR FACILITY.

"Iraq's Chemical and Biological Weapons"

General Wafiq al-Samarai Hussein Kamel, former head of Iraq's military intelligence, defected to the United States in 1994. He told American officials that as late as 1990 Iraq had produced VX on a large scale. He further stated that Iraq was capable of using VX in warfare.

United Nations weapons inspectors who entered Iraq after the Gulf War saw evidence that suggested Iraq had produced large quantities of anthrax, botulinum toxin, ricin, and aflatoxin (a poison made from fungus that causes liver damage). In 1996, the U.S. Department of Defense expressed American distrust of Iraq's statements about its chemical and biological weapons:

> **Iraq claims that all biological agents and munitions were unilaterally destroyed after the Gulf War. However, Iraq's record of misrepresentation and the lack of documentation to support these claims leave the status of Iraqi biological warfare stockpile in doubt . . .**

> **Another defector to the West, Lieutenant General Hussein Kamel, head of Iraq's biological weapons program and Saddam Hussein's son-in-law, also provided valuable information about Iraq's secret chemical and biological weapons programs. He returned to Iraq and was executed.**

stockpiles of chemical and biological weapons. Saddam Hussein expelled UNSCOM inspectors in November 1997.

In November 2002, the United Nations Security Council unanimously approved a strict new resolution to order Saddam Hussein to disarm. Resolution 1441 said that if Hussein did not disarm—that is, destroy facilities for making chemical and biological weapons and get rid of stockpiles—he would face "serious consequences." It was also rumored at this time that Hussein was trying to build a nuclear weapon—yet another reason for the U.N. resolution. U.S. President George W. Bush and British Prime Minister Tony Blair warned that the serious consequences would be delivered by American and British military troops. The U.N. resolution provided for a new team of weapons inspectors to enter Iraq on November 18, 2002.

UNSCOM inspectors entered Iraq, but could find no conclusive evidence that the country was producing weapons of mass destruction. As inspections dragged on, the United States and Great Britain pushed for a United Nations resolution that would allow a "coalition" of countries to invade Iraq, topple Saddam Hussein's regime, and find and destroy chemical and biological weapons. The United Nations could not get enough member countries to agree to the proposed military action, so failed to order a resolution authorizing an invasion of Iraq. Despite the fact that a U.N. resolution to authorize military action against Iraq had not been passed, a coalition consisting of approximately 300,000 military troops, primarily from the United States, Great Britain, and Australia, entered Iraq from Kuwait on March 19, 2003. The Coalition troops moved quickly to Baghdad. Iraqi forces offered some resistance, but military objectives were quickly met. By mid- to late-April, major cities in Iraq were largely under Coalition control, and Saddam Hussein's regime had toppled. As of June 2003, Coalition troops remained in Iraq to keep order, search for chemical and biological weapons, and locate former members of Saddam Hussein's government.

The Coalition

According to a March 21, 2003, White House press release, contributions from Coalition members ranged from direct military participation, to humanitarian and reconstruction aid, to political support. The forty-six countries publicly committed to the Coalition included:

Afghanistan	El Salvador	Kuwait	Panama	Spain
Albania	Eritrea	Latvia	Philippines	Turkey
Australia	Estonia	Lithuania	Poland	Uganda
Azerbaijan	Ethiopia	Macedonia	Portugal	United Kingdom
Bulgaria	Georgia	Marshall Islands	Romania	United States
Colombia	Honduras	Micronesia	Rwanda	Uzbekistan
Costa Rica	Hungary	Mongolia	Singapore	
Czech Republic	Iceland	Netherlands	Slovakia	
Denmark	Italy	Nicaragua	Solomon Islands	
Dominican Republic	Japan	Palau	South Korea	

The speculation at this time was that Saddam Hussein had either been killed in a Coalition bombing raid, or had fled the country. By June 2003, however, Coalition forces had received several reports claiming that Saddam Hussein and his two sons were alive and in hiding in Iraq.

While the Coalition forces' military objectives had largely been accomplished by June 2003, the Coalition troops remaining in Iraq to keep order and continue the search for weapons of mass destruction still faced armed resistors. Anticoalition snipers and suicide bombers killed thirteen American and British soldiers after peacekeeping efforts began. The search for evidence of chemical and biological weapons programs was intensified, but as of mid-June 2003, no conclusive evidence of such weapons in Iraq had been found.

9
Cheaters and Remedies

Iraq is not the only country that has continued to produce chemical and biological weapons, despite signing and ratifying the BTWC. (Iraq signed the BTWC in 1972, but didn't ratify it until 1991, and then only as a condition of the Gulf War cease-fire agreement.) The international community has gathered evidence suggesting that Iran, Syria, Egypt, North Korea, Libya, Israel, China, and Russia also have continued to produce chemical and biological weapons, in violation of the BTWC.

Most of these countries have denied that they have continued to produce such weapons. Due to the nature of their closed societies, no one has been allowed in to inspect for chemical and biological weapons. Former Russian President Boris Yeltsin declared in 1992 that his country would destroy or convert to other uses its biological weapons research and production facilities. But since four bioresearch centers in Russia are still off-limits to outsiders, the rest of the world has no way of confirming that biological weapons are no longer a priority for Russian weapons research and production.

When inspections are not allowed to determine whether or not a country has chemical and biological weapons, other nations usually assume they do. Even if inspections are allowed, they may be inconclusive, since equipment for producing toxic chemicals and pathogen cultures may be hidden or quickly converted to legitimate use. Other signs, however, can indicate that a country is producing or preparing to produce chemical and biological weapons. These signs include:

- **satellite photos that show excessive security around buildings proclaimed pharmaceutical factories, vaccine research laboratories, or other harmless facilities;**

- **indications that a nation has purchased or attempted to purchase large quantities of chemical weapon ingredients, biological organism cultures, growth media, or other materials used in the manufacture of chemical and biological weapons;**

- **notation that a country is exporting equipment or supplies used in programs to manufacture chemical and biological weapons;**

- **attempted recruitment of Russian scientists to aid in the development of chemical and biological weapons programs;**

- **the reported or rumored theft of large amounts of material needed in chemical and biological weapons production;**

- **indications by soil or wastewater testing, environmental observations, and other reports that a plant is producing CBWs;**

• reports of an unusually large number of deaths of animals and/or people in an area due to disease or toxic chemical exposure. Such reports can mean that chemical or biological agents have been released in an area, either by accident or to test an agent;

• the verification by **UNSCOM** investigators that CBWs were used in a war or conflict, as in the Iran-Iraq War in the 1980s;

• testimony by defectors detailing chemical and biological programs of the countries they fled.

Here is what is known (such as treaties signed, existing technology, and former use of CBWs) or suspected about chemical and biological weapons programs in eight countries, mostly in the Middle East:

	Iraq	Iran	Syria	Egypt	Libya	Israel	North Korea	China
Signed BTWC	Yes	No	Yes	Yes	Yes	No	Yes	Yes
Ratified CWC	No	Yes	No	No	No	No	No	Yes
Has Chemical Weapons	Yes	Yes	Yes	Yes	Yes	Yes	Yes	Yes
Has Biological Weapons	Yes	Probably	Probably	Probably	No	Yes	Yes	Probably
Has Technology and Infrastructure to Support CBWs	Yes	Yes	Yes	Yes	No	Yes	Yes	Yes
Has Used Chemical and/or Biological Weapons	Yes—1980–1988 against Iran	No	No	Yes—1963 against Yemen	Yes—War with Chad	No	No	No

Those countries that have continued to mass-produce chemical and biological weapons do so mostly because:

- **they fear that a more powerful country will use aggression against them, and actually using or threatening to use chemical and biological weapons can be an effective deterrent;**

- **they want to intimidate, dominate, or capture close neighbors, and believe chemical and biological weapons could help their cause;**

- **they want to intimidate or eliminate anti-government elements within their own borders.**

Some experts worry that the efforts of the Bill Clinton and George W. Bush administrations to bolster United States defenses against biological weapons will add to the threat of bioterrorism because much of the money allotted for this purpose will go to biotechnology and defense industries, leading to increases in the numbers of laboratories and scientists with access to bioterrorism research. But could these increases actually increase the threat?

Possibly, said Barbara Hatch Rosenberg in a February 2002 lecture at the Wilson School of Public and International Affairs at Princeton University. Rosenberg is a microbiologist and environmental research scientist at the State University of New York at Purchase and chairperson of the Federation of American Scientists' Chemical and Biological Arms Control Program. She said she is concerned about an "enormous increase" in money from the federal government for research into bioterrorism agents because this will cause too many scientists and laboratories to enter the field, making the program difficult to oversee.

The number of researchers and laboratories should be tightly controlled, Rosenberg said, instead of the large

"Protecting Against Chemical and Biological Weapons"

Wayne Landis, Director of the Institute of Environmental Toxicology, Huxley College of the Environment, Western Washington University in Bellingham, Washington, says he speaks often to the public about protecting against chemical and biological weapons. Given no prior warning of an attack, there is not much the average citizen can do, Landis says. "Our government needs to make sure public health systems are well equipped and prepared, and primary caregivers should be well trained to recognize symptoms, since many health care workers have never seen smallpox, or even measles or mumps."

According to Landis, governments can also make sure that those countries that have chemical and biological weapons destroy them (as the United Nations hoped to do in Iraq in 2003), and that nations do not acquire the materials they need to make chemical and biological weapons. (This is difficult, however, because of beneficial uses for many of these agents.)

Most private citizens will not be protected from a chemical or biological weapon by ineffective gas masks purchased at army surplus stores or paint masks lacking the proper filters. "To be truly protected," Landis says, "you have to be covered from head to toe, and this is difficult for the average person."

Fortunately, Landis continues, "With gas exposure, symptoms show up quickly, and most chemical agents fade away quickly. If you survive the first several minutes of exposure [to a chemical weapon], you are not likely to die. At this point, take off your clothes and wash yourself with soap, using lots of water."

If possible, of course, the best protection against exposure to chemical or biological weapons is to be forewarned so that you can leave the area.

THE TYVEK PROTECH "F," LEFT, AND THE CLEAR HAZMAT SUITS, RIGHT, ARE BOTH DESIGNED FOR PROTECTION AGAINST NUCLEAR, BIOLOGICAL, AND CHEMICAL INCIDENTS. THE TYVEK SUIT COSTS $49; THE CLEAR SUIT, USED BY THE ISRAELI ARMY, IS PRICED AT $150.

amounts of government money available for biodefense research being spread around to "a lot more people and a lot more laboratories around the country from which bioterrorists can emerge, as [the anthrax attacker] just did.

"By spreading around this access and this knowledge, we're asking for trouble," she added. (Rosenberg suspected that the anthrax terrorist was once employed as a government scientist.)

On the other hand, according to some experts, money spent on a strong defense against biological weapons may be the best deterrent. Tara O'Toole, director of the Johns Hopkins Center for Civilian Biodefense Strategies, told reporters in October 2002 that the threat of bioterrorism could increase over the next five years, unless the United States launches an extensive biodefense program, similar in funding and zeal to the Apollo space program of the 1960s.

"The notion that you can lock up the bugs, or that we can achieve biosecurity by watching scientists [who] are admittedly working on the bugs that we think in 2002 are most likely to be used as weapons, is very naïve," O'Toole said.

Those nations that follow the provisions of the BTWC and the CWC are no longer researching, producing, and stockpiling chemical and biological weapons. They are allowed under the two agreements, however, to research and develop defense mechanisms, such as vaccines, drugs, and protective gear. In fact, several billion dollars has been allotted by the George W. Bush administration to see that United States residents are protected.

Concerning biological weapons control, Barbara Hatch Rosenberg made these points in her testimony to the Subcommittee on National Security, Veterans Affairs and International Relations, House Committee on Government Reform, Hearing on the Biological Weapons Convention Protocol: Status and Implications, June 5, 2001:

1. The BTWC is still the world's best chance of controlling biological weapons, since it has been adjusted to include on-site inspections.

2. In addition to on-site inspections of suspected biological weapons facilities, BTWC-mandated global surveillance and control of emerging diseases can lessen the chance that biological weapons will be used or tested. This provision in the protocol attempts to give countries control in handling infectious diseases, and provides for global early warning of emerging diseases.

3. The ethical education of biological scientists can help them understand the implications of ongoing or future work. "There is little or no awareness of international concerns and prohibitions on the misuse of biology," Rosenberg said.

4. International self-monitoring of bioscience work would allow for non-government means to keep track of scientists' work with pathogens and other biologically active material. (Details of such a plan were not provided.)

Contrary to Rosenberg's remarks, some experts believe the BTWC is not the answer. The United States objected to the latest provisions in of the BTWC in 2001, thus tabling the matter indefinitely.

On the other hand, the CWC, with the cooperation of the chemical industry, has become increasingly effective, primarily through on-site inspections and the monitoring of equipment and chemical sales. Economic sanctions against offending nations are another way to discourage countries from producing and stockpiling chemical and biological weapons. Sanctions may include:

• withdrawal of all or a portion of foreign aid provided by other countries;

• Refusal to sell the materials needed to make CBWs, or a refusal to trade at all with the offending countries, which would include refusing to buy goods and materials from offending countries.

The threat posed by chemical and biological weapons is directly related to the nation's preparedness for such an attack. Of course, citizens can only be protected against chemical and biological weapons attacks in advance if they know the exact time and place the attack will occur, and this is highly unlikely. If such attacks occur against civilians, victims would have to rely on the country's public health network to obtain vaccinations, antidotes, drugs, and medical treatment.

The likelihood that civilians would have proper protective gear against chemical and biological weapons is slim, since they would need to wear the gear constantly or have it readily available at all times in order to prevent exposure to pathogens or toxic chemicals. Military troops anticipating a chemical or biological attack, however, would probably have donned protective gear and received vaccinations against organisms most likely to be used.

Eliminating chemical and biological weapons is a major challenge facing the international community. While steps have been taken to reveal violations and to pressure those countries that still produce chemical and biological weapons to stop their programs, the threat still exists. More work is needed to convince all countries that chemical and biological weapons have no place in human society.

10
Protecting Ourselves and the World

Unfortunately, there is little that private citizens can do to lessen the threat of a chemical or biological weapons attack. Knowledge of the limits and capabilities of those weapons and calm assessment of the risk they pose are helpful for peace of mind, but the government is the first line of defense against chemical and biological weapons. As Donald A. Henderson of the Johns Hopkins Center for Civilian Biodefense Strategies wrote in "The Looming Threat of Bioterrorism," *Science*, February 26, 1999, "Clearly there is growing public awareness of the threat of bioterrorism, and there is nascent concern among medical and public health professionals as well. This is important because if real progress is to be made in addressing this difficult problem, a substantially greater input of good science, medicine, and public health will be needed."

Our government continues diplomatic efforts to convince nations that have chemical and biological weapons to disarm, as seen in President George W. Bush's insistence on strict enforcement of United Nations resolution 1441 concerning Iraq's disarmament. In March 2003, the United States prepared to go to war against Iraq if that country did not significantly reduce the weapons of mass destruction it was believed to possess and to offer conclusive proof of the destruction of such weapons. Secretary of State Colin Powell told the United Nations that the U.S. government had reason to believe that Saddam Hussein's regime had moved materials for weapons of mass destruction around the country to hide them from U.N. inspectors, had destroyed only a small number of its total stockpile of banned missiles, and was secretly creating backup facilities to produce more.

"Unfortunately, the inspection effort isn't working," Powell said in a speech making the United States' case for military action to disarm Iraq. "Nothing we have seen . . . indicates Saddam Hussein has taken the strategic and political decision to disarm."

While the United States considered military action to force disarmament in Iraq, the government also funded programs to help protect American citizens from the effects of attack by chemical or biological weapons. For instance, the government-funded smallpox vaccination program and other efforts to improve our nation's response to emergencies, such as establishment of the Homeland Security Department, were evidence in 2003 that the U.S. government is concerned about the threat of chemical and biological weapons.

While governments grope for solutions to the problems posed by the production and possible use of chemical and biological weapons, they continue to keep chemical agents on hand for crowd and riot control, a measure that is permitted by international agreements. In one recent incident, such an agent was used to subdue terrorists in Russia, creating a controversial situation where some nations believed Russia acted illegally or, at the least, inhumanely.

On October 23, 2002, Chechen guerrillas overran a theater in Moscow. They demanded that Russian troops leave Chechnya, a small Russian province. A performance of a Russian hit musical "North-East" (*Nord-Ost*) was halfway over when more than fifty men and women with explosives strapped to their bodies stormed the theater. For the next fifty-eight hours, the guerrillas held hostage some 850 performers and theater-goers, many of them children. As the siege wore on, Russian military Special Forces surrounded the theater, but the guerrillas did not surrender. When shots were fired inside the building, the Russian government decided to take action. Soldiers piped gas through air vents into the theater. The gas disabled both the guerrillas and the hostages, allowing the soldiers to move in. Guerrillas, even those knocked out by the gas, were shot, and hostages were removed.

When the standoff ended early in the morning of October 26 and casualties were totaled, all but four of the guerrillas (two escaped and two were arrested) and 115 hostages were dead. The Chechens shot two hostages and 113 apparently died from the gas. More than 200 hostages were hospitalized, some in critical condition. The Russian government refused, at first, to say what type of gas. Some Western experts thought it was BZ, a nerve gas, but physicians at a Western embassy in Moscow who were allowed to examine the bodies of the dead hostages believed it to have been opium-based.

A week after the tragedy, the Russian government finally admitted that the gas used was an opiate. Opiates act as anesthetics, causing sleepiness and unconsciousness. In high dosages, however, these drugs can cause coma, respiratory and circulatory failure, and death. Used inside the theater, and in high concentrations, observers theorized that the gas overwhelmed the respiratory systems of those who died.

The governments of some nations also speculated that the gas used by Russian troops to subdue the Chechen guerrillas was part of the large stockpile of chemical weapons still maintained in Russia. Other nations, however, maintained that the Russians did not act illegally, since no agreement prohibits the use and development of chemical agents for purposes of riot control.

To comply with the CWC, Russia agreed to destroy all chemical weapons stockpiles by 2007. A lack of money for destruction of the weapons has halted the destruction process, and it is doubtful that Russia can meet the 2007 deadline.

Three issues are likely to significantly influence chemical and biological defense in the twenty-first century:

1. The global proliferation of biological weapons, if nations continue to violate the CWC and the BTWC.

2. Advances in technology that will affect the development of chemical and biological weapons and defenses against them.

3. Changes in the future use of chemical and biological weapons

By February 1993, the Gulf War had ended and the Union of Soviet Socialist Republics (U.S.S.R.) had broken up. A panel of the U.S. House of Representatives Committee on Armed Services submitted a report, "Special Inquiry of the House Armed Services Committee into the Chemical and Biological Weapons Threat." The report stated that the total amount of chemical weapons in the world had decreased, but the situations where toxic chemicals might be used had increased. The new threat was largely from Third World countries, the report claimed, which meant that U.S. military forces deployed in these countries could conceivably face attack from chemical and biological weapons.

Since 1993, the threat of the use of chemical and biological weapons by disgruntled nations or terrorist groups has remained the same as reported. Those nations attempting to meet the provisions of the CWC and BTWC have worked to reduce their production facilities and stockpiles, while, unfortunately, some nations continue to pursue research and development of CBWs. The emphasis in those nations that have dismantled their chemical and biological weapons facilities or converted them to legitimate uses is on protective measures such as the following:

• scientists are working to make vaccinations safer, and to develop a multi-purpose vaccine that would protect a person against more than one pathogen;

• respirators and facemasks are lighter and vastly more effective than those available in the past. Today's respirators have dual filters and are battery-operated. Filters and batteries can be changed without removing the mask;

• biohazard suits and other protective gear, such as respirators and facemasks, have been improved and are now available to the general public, as well as the military, (although detailed advance warning would be necessary for civilians to don the suits in time to protect themselves against chemical or biological weapons attacks;)

• antidotes effective against various nerve gases and other chemicals are available in some cases;

• new drugs, such as anti-viral drugs, are being developed to effectively treat a wider variety of biological agents.

Many developed nations, including the United States, Great Britain, and Japan, are active in efforts to control the spread of chemical and biological weapons, through the rigorous monitoring of countries suspected of making CBWs and through the imposition of sanctions against those countries. Provisions of the CWC and the BTWC have also helped in the international community's attempts to monitor and schedule for destruction production facilities and stockpiles of chemical and biological weapons. The United Nations Monitoring, Verification and Inspection Commission (UNMOVIC), established by United Nations resolution, has sent inspection teams to Iraq, but has not yet been used as extensively as it might be in the future. UNMOVIC inspections, together with punitive sanctions, could be the world's best hope for eliminating chemical and biological weapons. Both chemical and biological weapons require precursors, and tracking the sale or theft of these precursors may help detect covert programs.

The chemical and biological weapons threat can also change in the future as biotechnology continues to advance. Theoretically, disease-causing biological agents can be genetically altered to increase potency and to escape detection.

The CBWs threat may also change as the agents are used differently. Currently, no one can accurately estimate the chances of civilians facing a chemical or biological attack. The threat may increase in the future, however, if the following conditions exist:

- **military troops are able to better protect themselves through vaccinations, improved drugs and antidotes, improved detection devices, and protective gear, while civilians are seen as an unprotected target;**

- **problems with the delivery systems of chemical and biological weapons are solved, so that large amounts of the agents can be widely disseminated;**

• nations no longer engage in widespread wars, but instead prefer a series of terrorist attacks.

According to Jessica Stern, author of *The Ultimate Terrorists*, the following measures can help prevent a build-up of chemical and biological weapons and help protect against attack by such weapons:

1. Create an emergency fund to be used for helping countries that have sustained chemical or biological attacks.

2. Help Russia secure its chemical and biological weapons and facilities.

3. Improve protection of the United States and its foreign borders.

4. Help former scientists, guards, and others who worked in government chemical and biological weapons programs find civilian employment (especially in countries like Russia, where such workers need gainful employment to support themselves and their families).

5. Increase funding for research and development of protective measures against, and accurate detection of, chemical and biological weapons.

6. Improve international sharing of information. Create hotlines and electronic databases that are available to intelligence and law enforcement agencies, so that terrorists and their activities can be tracked, warnings can be issued, help can be requested, and authorities consulted.

"Reacting to Disaster"

The American Red Cross says that our reactions to disasters caused by humans, such as the September 11, 2001, terrorist attacks, are more severe than reactions to natural disasters like floods and hurricanes. In an online activity sheet titled, "Why Do I Feel Like This?" the Red Cross offers these reasons for the stress we feel after a terrorist attack:

Lack of warning. If we can prepare to protect ourselves, in ways such as boarding up windows when a hurricane warning is in force, we are less likely to be frightened.

Abrupt changes in our normal routine. We felt safe before the terrorist attacks, but we no longer feel safe afterward.

Type of destructive agent. Guns, for instance, may be less frightening than bombs or chemical and biological weapons to some people. (Or individuals may fear all destructive agents equally.)

Fear of more attacks. We believe that since a destructive attack happened once, it can happen again.

Outcome of rescue attempts. Our fear increases as many people die in an attack and even rescue workers are not safe. We can even feel guilty because we survived, and perhaps suffer posttraumatic stress days, weeks, months, and even years after the destructive event.

Media. When we see accounts of the destructive event over and over on television, or read about it daily in newspapers, we suffer anxiety that doesn't go away. Or, to protect ourselves from continuing anxiety, we may eventually have no reaction at all.

It is normal to be frightened and to suffer anxiety and stress after a human-caused disaster. Most of us recover within four to six weeks and are able to resume normal activities, but some studies show that it is not necessarily abnormal to feel disturbed even a year after a disaster such as September 11, 2001. Any young person who feels he or she cannot get over disastrous events without help should talk about the situation to a counselor, parent, or other trusted adult.

7. Update international and domestic laws regulating the production and stockpiling of chemical and biological weapons. The BTWC should be updated to include tougher monitoring requirements. Although the United States requires holders of certain biological agents to register with the CDC, nothing prevents individuals from isolating pathogens from nature. (Some experts have recommended that Congress pass legislation making it illegal to sell books and manuals that give instructions for mixing toxic chemicals, growing pathogens, or making bombs. Others say this would infringe upon the freedom of speech in the United States.) Also at risk is curtailing the peaceful, helpful use of biological technologies in our zeal to control bioweapons.

While some of the measures discussed in these chapters can help us have peace of mind, nothing can completely rid the world of the threat of chemical and biological weapons. Living with this threat may simply be necessary in the dangerous world we inhabit. We hope that, working together, nations can force those countries known to have chemical and biological weapons to disarm. Sanctions against countries that continue to develop chemical and biological weapons may also help lessen the threat that the weapons will be used.

In the United States, we can encourage our elected representatives to make sure the government is prepared to deal with chemical or biological weapons attacks. Can we treat the injured, protect those who will be first responders in a chemical or biological emergency, and otherwise respond quickly, compassionately, and with justice in the event of an attack with chemical or biological weapons? We hope so, but only time will tell.

Notes

Chapter 1

pp. 9–11, The Johns Hopkins Center for Civilian Biodefense Strategies, "Dark Winter," http://www.hopkins-biodefense.org/darkwinter.html. (Accessed September 10, 2002.)

pp. 15–19, 22, Bobbitt, Luke, Ben Johnson, and Ryan Smith. "Bio/Chemical Weapons: Transparent Problems, Hidden Solutions," http://www.davison.k12.mi.us/academic/luke.htm. (Accessed September 20, 2002.)

Mayer, Lt. Col. Terry N. USAF. "The Biological Weapon: A Poor Nation's Weapon of Mass Destruction," *Air & Space Chronicles.* http://www.airpower.maxwell.af.mil/airchronicles/battle/chp8.html. (Accessed September 20, 2002.)

Pitcavage, Mark. "Afraid of Bugs: Assessing our Attitudes Towards Biological and Chemical Terrorism," *The Militia Watchdog,* February 12, 1999. http://www.militia-watchdog.org/anthrax.htm. (Accessed September 20, 2002.)

Croddy, Eric. *Chemical and Biological Warfare: A Comprehensive Survey for the Concerned Citizen.* New York: Copernicus Books, 2002, p. 127.

pp. 20–21, Tucker, Jonathan B., ed., *Toxic Terror.* Cambridge, MA: MIT Press; Jessica Eve Stern, "Larry Wayne Harris—(1998)," pp. 227–246.

Chapter 2

pp. 23–27, "Anthrax Fact File," BBC News
http://news.bbc.co.uk.hi/english/static/in_depth/world/2002/
anthrax/default.stm
(Accessed September 10, 2002.)

pp. 27–28, Haney, Daniel Q. "Treating Anthrax Victim Was
Difficult," *Detroit News*, October 26, 2001, pp. 1, 2
http://www.ph.ucla.edu/epi/bioter/treatinganthraxdifficult.html.
(Accessed September 11, 2002.)
Contreras, Joseph, Michael Isikoff, and Howard Fineman. "Anthrax
Alarm," *Newsweek* Web Exclusive, October 8, 2001, p. 3
http://www.msnbc.com/news/639937.asp.
(Accessed September 10, 2002.)

pp. 29–31, 32, "Chronology of Anthrax Events," *South Florida Sun-Sentinel*
http://www.sun-sentinel.com/news/local/southflorida/
sfl-1013anthraxchronology.story?coll=sfla-home-headlines.
(Accessed September 10, 2002.)
"Chronology of Anthrax-Related Events," *Poughkeepsie Journal*,
October 28, 2001
http://www.poughkeepsiejournal.com/projects/attack/co102801s5.shtml.
(Accessed September 11, 2002.)
(Text of letters) FBI Web site: http://www.fbi.gov/pressrel/
pressrel01/102301.htm (Accessed September 12, 2002.)

p. 32–35, Leslie Gaffney, "Bioterrorism and the Need for Education," *Onward*,
December 13, 2001.
http://pages.emerson.edu/students/Leslie_Gaffney/jr681/
bioterrorism/printer.html. (Accessed September 11, 2002.)
Interview with Dr. Richard Pilch, October 8, 2002.
Croddy, Eric. *Chemical and Biological Warfare: A
Comprehensive Survey for the Concerned Citizen*. New York:
Copernicus Books, 2002, p. 195.

pp. 33, 36, Bowman, Lee. Scripps Howard News Service, "Vaccine Plan
Has Experts Concerned," *Rapid City Journal*, November 9, 2002,
p. A5.

Chapter 3

p. 41, Miller, Judith, Stephen Engelberg, and William Broad.
Germs: Biological Weapons and America's Secret War. New
York: Simon & Schuster, 2001, pp. 43, 44.

pp. 42–50, Alibek, Ken. *Biohazard*. New York: Random House, 1999,
pp. 164–166.

Fact Sheets on Anthrax, Botulinum Toxin, Plague, Smallpox, Tularemia, and VHF: Johns Hopkins Center for Civilian Biodefense Strategies http://www.hopkins-biodefense.org/pages/agents/. (Accessed September 16, 2002.)

Osterholm, Michael T., and John Schwartz. *Living Terrors: What America Needs to Know to Survive the Coming Bioterrorist Catastrophe.* New York: Delacorte Press, 2000, pp. 14–23.

Rainbow Pediatrics Knowledgebase, "Biological & Chemical Warfare and Terrorism." http://www.rainbowpediatrics.net/faq/24.13.html. (Accessed September 20, 2002.)

pp. 50–52, *Germs: Biological Weapons and America's Secret War*, pp. 15–33.

Chapter 4

pp. 54–58, *Living Terrors: What America Needs to Know to Survive the Coming Bioterrorist Catastrophe.* New York: Delacourte Press, 2000, pp. 50, 51.

John W. Morehead, "Religious Terrorism—Apocalypse Now: Armageddon Enters the New Age of Terrorism," *Watchman Expositor* http://www.watchman.org/reltop/religiousterror.htm. (Accessed September 19, 2002.)

Olson, Kyle B. "Aum Shinrikyo: Once and Future Threat?" *Emerging Infectious Diseases*, July–August, 1999 http://www.cdc.gov/ncidod/EID/vol5no4/olson.htm. (Accessed September 18, 2002.)

BBC News, "Cult Leader Trial Resumes in Japan," May 23, 2002 http://news.bbc.co.uk/2/hi/asia-pacific/2004000.stm (Accessed September 19, 2002.)

pp. 58–63, "Chemical Warfare Agents," *SIPRI Chemical and Biological Warfare Project*, August 18, 1998, updated September 17, 2001 http://projects.sipri.se/cbw/cbw-agents/mainpage.html. (Accessed September 18, 2002.)

Croddy, Eric. *Chemical and Biological Warfare: A Comprehensive Survey for the Concerned Citizen.* New York: Copernicus Books, 2000, pp. 98, 105–109, 112–114, 116, 117.

Chapter 5

pp. 64–66, 68–69, "History of Chemical Warfare and Current Threat," Medical NBC Online. http://www.nbc-med.org/. (Accessed September 24, 2002.)

"History of Biological Warfare and Current Threat," Glasgow Life Saving and First Aid Crew. http://www.glasgowfirstaid.org/disaster/biological/history_of_chemical_warfare.htm. (Accessed September 24, 2002.)

Croddy, Enc. *Chemical and Biological Warfare: A Comprehensive Survey for the Concerned Citizen.* New York: Copernicus Books, 2002, pp. 127, 128, 207, 208.

Osterholm, Michael T., and John Schwartz. *Living Terrors: What America Needs to Know to Survive the Coming Bioterrorist Catastrophe.* New York: Delacorte Press, 2000, p. 68.

"Chemical Weapons History," MDB's Chemical Weapons Index http://www.geocities.com/CapeCanaveral/Lab/4239/ chemweapons/history.html(Accessed September 24, 2002.)

"A History of Chemical Warfare," Greg Goebel's Worldscapes http://www.vectorsite.net/twgas2.html. (Accessed September 25, 2002.)

p. 67, *Medical Aspects of Chemical and Biological Warfare* in *Textbooks of Military Medicine.* Ed. Brig. Gen. R. Zajtchuk, M.C., U.S. Army. Office of the Surgeon General, Dept. of the Army, U.S.A. 1997, Introduction. Available online at Borden Institute's *Textbooks of Medicine* site.

http://www.bordeninstitute.army.mil/cwbw/default_index.htm (Accessed October 1, 2002.)

pp. 69–70, Ibid, p. 97, p. 101 (table).

p. 71, "Chemical and Biological Weapons," OneWorld.net http://www.oneworld.net/guides/cbweapons/front.shtml. (Accessed September 19, 2002.)

p. 72, Croddy, Enc. *Chemical and Biological Warfare: A Comprehensive Survey for the Concerned Citizen.* New York: Copernicus Books, 2002, pp. 224–225.

p. 76, Achieng, Judith. "Politics: UN Sends Doctors to Treat Survivors of Toxic Chemicals," Inter Press Service, August 2, 1999. http://www.oneworld.org/ips2/august99/23_42_085.html. (Accessed September 26, 2002.)

Medical Aspects of Chemical and Biological Warfare, p. xi.

Croddy, *Chemical and Biological Warfare: A Comprehensive Survey for the Concerned Citizen,* pp. 175, 238–248.

p. 77, "Gulf War Syndrome," *Expanded Columbia Electronic Encyclopedia* http://www.historychannel.com/perl/ print_book.pl?ID=90264. (Accessed September 25, 2002.)

"Biological Warfare," http://www.historychannel.com/perl/ print_book.pl?ID=75655. (Accessed September 25, 2002.)

pp. 77–78, Croddy, Enc. *Chemical and Biological Warfare: A Comprehensive Survey for the Concerned Citizen,* pp. 162, 164.

Chapter 6

pp. 79, 80, Alibek, Ken. *Biohazard.* New York: Random House, 1999, p. ix.

pp. 81, "History of Chemical Warfare and Current Threat," Medical NBC Online
http://www.nbc-med.org. (Accessed September 24, 2002.)
pp. 81–83, *Biohazard*, pp. 70-80.
Croddy, *Chemical and Biological Warfare: A Comprehensive Survey for the Concerned Citizen*. New York: Copernicus Books, 2002, p. 32.
p. 83, "Chemical Weapons Tests Exposures Revealed," *DAV Magazine*, 2002 July/August
http://www.dav.org/magazine/2002-4/Chemical_Weapons2053. (Accessed October 2, 2002.)
Croddy, *Chemical and Biological Warfare: A Comprehensive Survey for the Concerned Citizen*. New York: Copernicus Books, 2002, pp. 213–216.
pp. 83–84, Matt Kelley, Associated Press, "Chemical Weapons Tests by US in 60s," *Yahoo! News*, October 9, 2002 http://story.news.yahoo.com/news?tmpl=story2&cid=542&u=/ap/20021009/ap_on_go_ca_ (Accessed October 9, 2002.)
pp. 84–85, "A History of Secret Human Experimentation," Health News Network, 1998-2000, pp. 1, 2.
http://www.healthnewsnet.com/humanexperiments.html. (Accessed October 9, 2002.)
pp. 86–87, Miller, Engelberg, and Broad. *Germs: Biological Weapons and America's Secret War*. New York: Simon & Schuster, 2001, pp. 186, 187.

Chapter 7

pp. 89–90, 92–95, *Medical Aspects of Chemical and Biological Warfare* in *Textbooks of Military Medicine*. Ed. Brig. Gen. R. Zajtchuk, M.C., U.S. Army. Office of the Surgeon General, Dept. of the Army, U.S.A. 1997, Introduction. Available online at Borden Institute's *Textbooks of Medicine* site, pp. 91, 92–105.
http://www.bordeninstitute.army.mil/cwbw/default_index.htm (Accessed October 1, 2002)
Le Masque à Gaz, "Who Invented the First Gas Mask?", "The Early Masks of W.W.I." "The New Developments of World War II," "The Korean War and Vietnam," "Trouble in the Persian Gulf."
http://www.nofuture.com/Imag/history/history.htm. (Accessed October 1, 2002.)
from same Web site: "The Early Gas Masks of World War I."

Chapter 8

p. 96, Stern, Jessica. *The Ultimate Terrorists*. Cambridge, MA.: Harvard University Press, 2001, p. 69.
p. 97, Croddy, Eric. *Chemical and Biological Warfare: A Comprehensive Survey for the Concerned Citizen*, New York: Copernicus Books, 2002, p. 21.

pp. 98–99, preamble quote: Alibek, Ken. *Biohazard*, front page before Table of Contents.

"Convention on the Prohibition of the Development, Production and Stockpiling of Bacteriological (Biological) and Toxin Weapons and on their Destruction" United Nations Office of Geneva http://www.unog.ch/frames/disarm/distreat/bac_72.htm. (Editor: bac_72.htm.) (Accessed October 15, 2002.) Major International Instruments on Disarmament and Related Issues: http://www.unog.ch/frames/disarm/distreat/warfare.htm. (Accessed September 19, 2002.)

pp. 99–100, Miller, Engelberg, & Broad. *Germs: Biological Weapons and America's Secret War.* New York: Simon & Schuster, 2001, p. 136. Osterholm and Schwartz, *Living Terrors: What America Needs to Know to Survive the Coming Bioterrorist Catastrophe,* p. 41.

pp. 100–101, *Germs*, 137, pp. 223–255.

p. 102 (OPCW), Croddy, p. 237, pp. 245, 246.

p. 104(Harris), Osterholm and Schwartz, *Living Terrors*, pp. 60, 61. Jonathan B. Tucker, *Toxic Terror: Assessing Terrorist Use of Chemical and Biological Weapons.* Cambridge, MA: MIT Press, 2001, pp. 227–246.

pp. 106–107, Pilch interview.

pp. 107–108, *The Ultimate Terrorists.* p. 126. Croddy, p. 40.

pp. 108, 110, Edith M. Lederer, Associated Press, "Iraq Resolution Approved Unanimously," *Rapid City Journal*, November 9, 2002, p. A5.

p. 111, The White House, President George W. Bush, "Operation Iraqi Freedom," March 21, 2003 http://www.whitehouse.gov/news/releases/2003/03/print/ 20030321-4.html. (Accessed May 6, 2003.)

Chapter 9

p. 112, Croddy, Enc. *Chemical and Biological Warfare: A Comprehensive Survey for the Concerned Citizen.* New York: Copernicus Books, 2002, p. 35.

p. 113, Ibid., p. 40. Miller, Engelberg, & Broad. *Germs: Biological Weapons and America's Secret War.* New York: Simon & Schuster, 2001, p. 185.

p. 114, Steven R. Bowman, "CRS Issue Brief for Congress, IB94029: Chemical Weapons Convention: Issues for Congress," Congressional Research Service. September 20, 2000, pp. 5, 6 http://enie.org/NLE/CRSreports/Waste/waste-25.cfm. (Accessed October 28, 2002.)

pp. 115–118, Joseph Dee, "Expert: Anthrax Suspect ID'd," *New Jersey Times*, February 19, 2002. http://www.nj.com/mercer/times/index.ssf?/mercer/times/ 02-10-IZAR1IUB.html. (Accessed May 5, 2003.)

pp. 118–119, Joan Lowy, Scripps Howard News Service, "Debate

Flares Over Bioterror Research," *Rapid City Journal,*
October 6, 2002, p. E9.
"Testimony of Barbara Hatch Rosenberg" House Committee on
Government Reform
http://www.house.gov/reform/ns/107th_testimony/
testimony_of_barbara_hatch_rosen.html. (Accessed October 25, 2002.)
p. 116, Author's interview with Wayne Landis, October 2002.

Chapter 10

p. 122, Jim Drinkard, "Powell: Intelligence Says Iraq is Deceiving,"
USA Today, March 6, 2003, p. 1A.
p. 123, Christian Caryl and Eve Conant, "Show of Nerve," *Newsweek,*
November 4, 2002, pp. 44, 45.
Maria Golovnina, "Russia Siege Funerals Start; Gas Linked to
Opiate," Reuters Yahoo! News, October 29, 2002:
http://story.news.yahoo.com/news?tmpl=story/u/nm/ 20021029/
wl_nm/russia_siege_dc_86. (Accessed October 29, 2002.)
pp. 127, 129, Stern, pp. 156–159.
p. 128, "Why Do I Feel Like This?" American Red Cross, 2001:
http://www.redcross.org/services/disaster/keepsafe/terror.html.
(Accessed October 29, 2002).

Further Information

For Further Reading

Cobb, Allan B. *Biological and Chemical Weapons: The Debate over Modern Warfare*. New York: Rosen Group, 2000.

Levine, Herbert M. *Chemical and Biological Weapons in Our Times*. Danbury, CT: Franklin Watts, 2001.

Payan, Gregory. *Deadly Chemical Weapons: Anthrax and Sarin*. Danbury, CT: Children's Press, 2000.

Pringle, Laurence P. *Chemical and Biological Warfare: The Cruelest Weapons*, rev. ed. Berkeley Heights, NJ: Enslow Publishers, Inc., 2001.

Web Sites

The Center for Civilian Biodefense Strategies
http://www.hopkins-biodefense.org

The Center for Defense Information
http://www.cdi.org/issues/cbw

Centers for Disease Control and Prevention
http://www.bt.cdc.gov

The Federation of American Scientists Chemical and Biological Arms Control Program
http://www.fas/bwc

The Henry L. Stimson Center
http://www.stimson.org/cwc

MILNET: Chemical and Biological Weapons
http://www.milnet.com/milnet/chembio.htm

Monterey Institute of International Studies
http://cns.miis.edu/research/cbw/possess.htm.
(Also at Monterey Institute of International Studies): Chemical and
Biological Weapons Resource Page
http://www.cns.miis.edu/research/cbw

Stockholm International Peace Research Institute: Educational Module
on Chemical and Biological Weapons
http://cbw.sipri.se

Bibliography

Alibek, Ken. *Biohazard*. New York: Random House, 1999.

Croddy, Eric. *Chemical and Biological Warfare: A Comprehensive Survey for the Concerned Citizen*. New York: Copernicus Books, 2002.

Frist, Bill. *When Every Moment Counts*. Lanham, MD: Rowman & Littlefield Publishers Inc., 2002.

Miller, Judith, Stephen Engelberg, and William Broad. *Germs: Biological Weapons and America's Secret War*. New York: Simon & Schuster, 2001.

Osterholm, Michael T., and John Schwartz. *Living Terrors: What America Needs to Know to Survive the Coming Bioterrorist Catastrophe*. New York: Delacorte Press, 2000.

Stern, Jessica. *The Ultimate Terrorists*. Cambridge, MA: Harvard University Press, 1999.

Tucker, Jonathan B. *Toxic Terror: Assessing Terrorist Use of Chemical and Biological Weapons*. Cambridge, MA: MIT Press, 2001.

Index

Page numbers in **boldface** are illustrations.

About the Author

Karen Judson lives with her husband in the Black Hills of South Dakota. She is a former college biology instructor and has also taught high school sciences, kindergarten, and grades one and three. She has written fifteen books for young adult readers. In her spare time she jogs, paints wildlife scenes, and designs quilts.